SECURITY MANUAL

SECURITY MANUAL

DAVID BROOKSBANK

GOWER

Published by
Gower Publishing Limited
Gower House
Croft Road
Aldershot
Hampshire
GU11 3HR
England

Gower Publishing Company
Suite 420
101 Cherry Street
Burlington
VT 05401-4405
USA

British Library Cataloguing in Publication Data is available from the British Library

Library of Congress Cataloging-in-Publication Data
Brooksbank, David.
Security manual / by David Brooksbank. -- 8th ed.
p.cm.
Includes bibliographical references and index.
ISBN-13: 978-0-566-08783-7
1. Industries--Security measures. 2. Industries--Secutiry measures--Great Britain. I. Title.
HV8290.B75 2007
65/8.4'73--dc22

2006100147

Printed and bound in Great Britain by TJ International Ltd, Padstow, Cornwall

Contents

List of Figures and Table

Foreword

It is pleasing indeed to welcome the eighth edition of the *Security Manual*, first written by John Wilson and Eric Oliver and currently revised and updated by David Brooksbank.

The role of the private security officer has developed considerably in recent years and ever higher standards of knowledge and performance are expected by employers and the public. The introduction of licensing and regulation, with its emphasis on training and qualifications aimed at achieving higher levels of professionalism, makes this publication even more relevant today.

Never before in our history has security had such a high profile in our everyday concerns. Vigilance and awareness coupled with intelligence-gathering and reporting are the first defences against those who threaten our communities, whether for the purposes of serious crime or terrorism. Security operatives are uniquely placed to help prevent incidents by exercising their powers of observation and appreciating they have a fundamental role in assisting the police and other agencies in ensuring public safety, as well as protecting the assets of their employers.

Every security officer and other person working in a security-related role – whether as a community support officer, warden, event steward or door supervisor – should find valuable information and guidance in this manual, which is relevant to their job and will help them to perform their duties in a more efficient and professional manner.

I recommend the *Security Manual* as an essential reference book for every security operative and supervisor. I hope that it will also help and encourage aspiring newcomers to enter the industry and pursue a career in what is a very diverse, rewarding and developing sector of the economy.

Patrick J Somerville, QPM,
International Chairman of IPSA and
Chairman of the Joint Security Industry Council (JSIC)

Preface to the Eighth Edition

More than three decades have passed since the first edition of this manual was written. The image and professionalism of the security officer and industry has changed immeasurably during that time. A uniformed security presence is now fully accepted as a reassuring sight in many public environments such as shopping centres and supermarkets. Moreover, security officers are accepted within business environments as being essential to the security of assets and the welfare of staff and visitors.

It is estimated that there are between 300 000 and 500 000 people working in the security industry and that the annual revenue of the UK's private security industry is £3–4 billion. In the coming years, the number of personnel is likely to grow as demands for professional security increase.

Since the previous edition of the *Security Manual*, many sectors of the security industry have come to be regulated by the Private Security Industry Act 2001. This legislation provided the statutory framework for the licensing of security staff in the United Kingdom, and legislated for the creation of the Security Industry Authority (SIA), charging it with managing the licensing of the private security industry as set out in the Act.

This manual, first published in 1969, has always been compiled with the objective of providing a ready source of practical reference and guidance for those working at the 'sharp end' of the security industry and those people who aspire to join the industry. The book has now been brought 'up to speed' to take into account the training needs of security officers and door supervisors licensed by the SIA. Its content will underpin the knowledge required in the study of recognised security qualifications and it will be a ready source of information for security managers and supervisors.

The expansion and regulation of the security industry has created many opportunities for those joining the industry. The possession of recognised qualifications – a requirement of licensing – will add to the other qualities expected of applicants. The security profession is, at last, regarded as an essential aide to crime reduction and public safety throughout the United Kingdom. The myth that to earn a decent living, the security employee has to work long hours has to be dispelled. In fact, career progression is available, and many supervisors and managers have been promoted through the ranks.

The background against which security operates has changed little over the years. We still have offences of robbery, burglary, organised shoplifting, fraud, violence, public disorder and, increasingly, the threat of terrorism. As regards the latter, the security industry has a significant role to play, and its management of CCTV systems has already contributed to inquiries into acts and attempted acts of terrorism. As the threat of terrorism continues, the role of the security officer will become even more significant.

One disturbing factor, not just for the security industry but for society too, is the increase in violent crime and its growing use by criminals on security staff and those likely to impede criminal acts. A new chapter on conflict resolution has therefore been included in the book. Other chapters have been updated to reflect changes to the law, in particular to fire safety and criminal law and procedure.

In compiling this new edition, thanks are due to Gary Seekins of the West Yorkshire Fire and Rescue Service for his advice and guidance in respect of the Regulatory Reform (Fire Safety) Order, to John Heald, Training Officer, West Yorkshire Police, for his guidance and interpretation of the new powers of arrest, to Lisa Harvey QPM, Diversity Trainer, West Yorkshire Police, for her guidance on cultural and diversity issues, and to the Security Service (MI5), who have allowed reproduction of some of their information on the terrorist threat.

Sadly, since the last edition, my co-author John Wilson has passed away. His contribution to the security industry and this manual cannot be underestimated. Up until his passing, John was satisfied that this manual, first written by him in 1969, should continue to be a ready source of information for the security professional.

At the time of this publication I will have completed 30 years police service. This I hope will free up more time to examine, analyse and contribute to the work of the security industry as well as conducting training sessions for security personnel.

In conclusion, the security industry is increasingly being accepted as a member of the wider 'police family', as it should be. Its expertise is being recognised as essential in the prevention of crime, disorder and terrorism. Licensing has been introduced and this can only be a good thing. However, it is suggested that up to 30 per cent of those working in the security industry do not meet the criteria, and in some sectors recruitment and retention remain a major problem, with a turnover rate of some 35 per cent, although this picture is changing.

Security is of great concern for business, and two in three companies now have a head of security and many now spend significantly more money on the protection of assets and staff than when this manual was last published.

The security industry is in good order and its retention of staff and its services will both improve. I hope that this publication will continue to assist in the educational needs of today's security personnel and be a ready source of information that is of everyday use to security officers, supervisors and managers.

David Brooksbank

1 Basics

'Security' is an occupation that encompasses many types of duty and skill. Even the terminology applied to its workforce varies, but in this manual the terms 'security officer' or 'professional' are preferred.

Security, in the sense of prevention of loss or injury, may be defined as 'the protection of assets of all kinds against loss from theft, fire, fraud, criminal acts or other injurious sources'. 'Property' is sometimes substituted for 'assets' but the latter is better because it includes confidential information and trade secrets that are important to their owner. There are marginal activities that need some poetic licence to fit into any abbreviated definition, such as the provision of security professionals for crowd control at sporting events, pop concerts and the like, where the cost of special duty police has become prohibitive.

Duties and responsibilities differ widely; security officers may provide out-of-hours static protection to a vulnerable site entirely on their own or they may be members of an organised force working regular shifts in a large industrial complex. In the former case the officer may well have been supplied by a contract security company and furnished with a sheet of instructions that apply to that particular site. In the latter they are likely to be working in accordance with much more detailed 'standing orders' laid down by the employer.

In the retail sphere of supermarkets, large stores and shopping precincts, security in the form of uniformed personnel is a visible deterrent to shoplifters and hooligans and gives confidence to customers and shop assistants alike. It also provides support for plain-clothes store detectives who are now more likely to be victims of violence than in the past. Owing to the growing tendency to sue for damages on the slightest pretext, a store detective needs thorough training in the legal considerations associated with making an arrest, because an unjustifiable action may be costly for the employer.

Few companies conduct their own cash carrying, sensibly making use of contract security companies equipped with purpose-built, radio-equipped vehicles, data tracking systems and trained crews. Such companies frequently diversify by transporting computer data and valuable packages. Most companies, however, concentrate on meeting guarding and patrolling requirements and there is a growing tendency, based on economic and administrative reasons, for them to be asked to supply uniformed personnel to supplement or replace in-house security staff for access control or routine patrolling.

As crime continues to grow, and with it fear, security has become more important in every sphere of life. Indeed, there is a public acceptance of the context of security. Quite apart from personnel, there has been a vast expansion in the manufacture and installation of burglar alarms, closed-circuit television (CCTV) and video recording, and in the installation of metal roller shutters and other forms of physical protection. In business, the value of regular risk assessment has been recognised as necessary to counter, among other threats, those of fraud, industrial espionage, disaster and terrorism.

This manual is designed not for specialists but for professionals involved in manned guarding, and also for supervisors and managers who are in day-to-day contact with fellow employees and the public, and who seek guidance to perform with confidence and efficiency. They require sufficient knowledge of the law, industrial relations and other relevant matters to be a company asset rather than a source of risk to their employer.

WHY SECURITY STAFF?

Skilled personnel are expensive to employ and the reasons for incurring the cost of employing security professionals are directly related to the foreseeable risks of not doing so. Electronic forms of protection, structural improvements and effective use of modern communication systems can reduce the numbers of security personnel that are necessary, but in many cases there is no substitute for making security personnel available. The following factors will influence the decision to employ security professionals:

- *Industrial and commercial.* To ensure the privacy of the premises and the business by excluding intruders, potential thieves, unwanted callers and other undesirables (access control).

- *Public demand.* A visible presence in shopping precincts and the like, to give confidence to customers by deterring hooliganism, violence, theft, drug taking and other sources of annoyance.

- *Insurers' insistence*. The presence of security professionals may be a condition of providing cover to premises, their contents and users. Research and governmental contracts may impose similar conditions.

- *Loss experience*. There may be unacceptable levels of theft or damage.

- *Impracticality*. There may be no other measures that are more suitable to the area being protected.

- *Risk limitation*. The prevention, detection and reporting of fire, theft, criminal damage, flooding, gas leaks and other hazards.

- *Necessary tasks with security implications*. The recording and controlling of vehicular traffic, visitor reception areas, out-of-hour's communications and enforcing company rules.

RECRUITMENT

People of all types and within a wide range of age groups may be acceptable as potential security professionals, providing they hold a Security Industry Authority licence and have certain qualities, including:

- integrity
- common sense
- ability and willingness to learn a new profession
- good health.

Objections to the wearing of a uniform may have to be overcome, and a change of relationship with fellow employees and members of the public is a factor that must be recognised. To employers a security professional may be seen as a representative of 'management' who is there to exercise discipline; to the public the security professional can no longer be a spectator at incidents but must be seen to act or lose respect and credibility. In addition, the hours of work may be long and unsocial.

The work of the security officer entails the following:

- shift and weekend working with socially inconvenient hours;
- the possibility of short-notice overtime working and shift changes;
- working alone on occasions;

- an element of personal risk of violence, for example, when carrying cash;
- using initiative when dealing with incidents that are not covered by instructions or training.

In-house security, where staff numbers and turnover are apt to be limited, offers little opportunity for internal promotion, but with the advent of examinations and recognised qualifications, career advancement may be possible in a wider field. Contract security is an expanding market where the need for competent supervisory staff will inevitably increase and those qualifications will prove invaluable.

There are few types of employee with the potential to cause so much trouble in so short a time for their employers as security staff. Officiousness, truculence, harassment and unjustified action against fellow employees may lead to industrial trouble. Any of these, or being rude or off-hand towards a customer or visitor, might alienate that person against the company and may result in lost business as well as generating a complaint against the security officer. If contract security is providing the service, its clients may terminate the agreement and serious cases of neglect of duty or misbehaviour could lead to legal action.

RESPONSIBILITIES

During the training of security officers, some mundane aspects of the job are not always emphasised to the extent they perhaps merit. The following lists of do's and don'ts, which are echoed later in the manual, may be helpful to a new officer and act as a reminder to his longer-serving colleagues.

Do not

- Act as if or imagine that you have the authority and powers of a police officer. A uniform identifies you but conveys no legal power beyond those of an ordinary citizen.
- Criticise management or its decisions to fellow employees or outsiders. Criticism may be repeated to your detriment and may be harmful to management and customers because security personnel are generally regarded as an authoritative source of information.
- Gossip about matters that are strictly 'security' issues; for example, observations on suspects or secreted property, suspicion about

individuals and weakness of security arrangements. Similarly, do not discuss confidential information about the company's activities that you acquire in the course of your work. This sort of gossip makes industrial espionage easy.

- Expect, solicit or accept favours from those with whom you come into contact in the course of your work. The offering of gifts is often the first step in involving a security professional in corrupt behaviour.

- Show favouritism, allow privileges or permit relaxation of instructions in respect of anyone, whether a fellow employee or an outsider.

- Lose your temper under provocation. It may make you act irrationally. Provocation or aggression is sometimes a deliberate ploy by offenders.

- Use obscene or abusive language when dealing with fellow employees, customers or the general public. Doing so exposes personal limitation and diminishes respect.

- Let yourself become bored to the detriment of your performance and your value to the employer. Boredom will soon show in your appearance and deportment, and may lead to you overlooking important matters where you should have taken action.

- 'Act the hero' in attempting something with no hope of success and certainty of injury. Use common sense. A good witness is infinitely more valuable than a brave but badly battered person who recollects nothing.

- Think that you have nothing more to learn about security work. When in doubt ask rather than risk making a fool of yourself.

There are of course other 'don'ts', but experience has shown that those listed are the most common sources of trouble.

Do

- Remember that the image you project is all-important in obtaining the respect of those with whom you come into contact. If you forfeit that respect, your job will be less pleasant and you will be less effective. Your dress, deportment, manner and appearance matter. It is important to look interested in what is happening around you and to be polite, patient and good-humoured when dealing with people.

- Always remember that goodwill is an important factor in your relationships. Be as helpful as you can, be consistent in your performance of the job and keep promises, otherwise you will risk creating a lasting grievance. Behave with clear impartiality and even-handedness.

- Study your company's rules and instructions until you are fully familiar with them.

- Consider your job and how you should behave in foreseeable circumstances. If you are in doubt about what action should be taken, ask in advance. Know where to find contingency plans for emergencies such as fire, bomb threats and explosions, and read them occasionally.

- Take notice of everything of a routine nature that occurs in your area of responsibility, including who does what, when, where and how. This will help you decide whether events or behaviour are unusual to the degree of meriting investigation.

- Learn from the mistakes and misfortunes of others. If you see anything in the media that could have a bearing on your work, discuss it with colleagues and superiors.

- Remember that your employer's interests are all-important, provided they are pursued within the law. Never give mistaken loyalty to a colleague who is behaving dishonestly or playing the fool. Such behaviour reflects badly on the whole security force.

- Ask if you do not know. Faced with an unforeseen problem, use your common sense to deal with it. If you think that security arrangements can be improved, do not hesitate to report or mention your suggestions.

There are times when security officers are alone in premises, and such occasions provide an excellent opportunity to examine the surroundings in detail. Contravention of health and safety legislation may be noticed or wastage identified. Such observations are to the employer's advantage and may in the long term instigate processes that will save the company money.

WHAT MIGHT BE ENCOUNTERED?

Occasionally, unusual incidents may occur that will attract the attention of senior management. How these are handled by the security staff will reflect the efficiency of both the security professional and the department as a whole. Such incidents could include the following:

- theft, fraud and false pretences
- fire or safety hazard
- criminal damage
- assault and wounding
- forgery
- drugs usage
- bribery and corruption
- sexual assault or harassment
- civil trespass
- hoax bomb calls and evacuation
- acts of terrorism.

These categories will be considered in detail in later chapters. For now it is enough to note that a security officer must have sufficient knowledge of the criminal law so as to avoid making mistakes that could prove costly to himself and his employer. Fires and accidents form a different category of incident from the others. The most common incident is theft (see Chapter 8). Theft automatically raises the question of powers of arrest (see Chapter 10) and, in the case of employees, management policy. Many companies always prosecute outsiders but exercise discretion in respect of their employees, preferring dismissal as a disciplinary sanction.

Considerations that are not discussed elsewhere in the manual but are nevertheless important to a security officer include the following:

- What discretion does the officer have to immediately involve the police? This would usually be in connection with persons arrested, break-ins, the presence or pursuit of suspects, serious thefts, assaults and the like requiring ambulance call-out, or other urgent matters.
- Who in management would make the decision to call the police? What is the company policy?
- Who would be informed or called out to incidents and in what sequence?
- Who will deal with enquiries from the media, either at the scene of an incident or with telephone requests for information? Security, unless authorised, should not take it upon itself to disclose information.

SECURITY AND POLICE

Security officers and the police have the same objectives, and any antipathy between them has been largely dissipated by the passage of time and common interests.

The security officer should act as an exemplary citizen and be as helpful as possible to the police. However, if instructions given by the employer involve illegal action, the excuse of 'acting under orders' will not exonerate the security officer from blame.

An employer's policy towards the reporting of offences and the prosecution of offenders may not be fully understood or agreed with, but must be accepted. There is no obligation for victims to report to the police offences that have been committed against them, or for that matter to prosecute known offenders.

Once a matter has been reported to the police, the police may insist on bringing proceedings. Factors an employer may take into account include the gravity of the loss, the inconvenience and time wastage of inquiries or court attendance, and the possibility of adverse publicity and mitigating circumstances in the case of employees. It should be noted that an employee or a visitor to premises who suffers loss can insist on the police being notified.

EMPLOYEE THEFT MOTIVATION

In the retail sector, employees are thought to be responsible for up to half of all losses. In industry and commerce, losses are not quantifiable but a permanent 'borrowing' of tools, calculators and similar equipment, stock shortages, petty pilfering and the like can only be attributable to employees.

An observant security professional who gets to know his fellow employees and listens to gossip may be able to identify a likely suspect for internal theft by being aware of the factors that may induce someone in employment to steal or commit damage. Some of the factors that might motivate employees to commit crime include:

- plain dishonesty and greed, or temptation created by finding a loophole in a vulnerable system;
- a grievance against the employer;
- external financial troubles and pressures including:
  (a) financial overcommitment, (b) sexual involvement with

another, (c) gambling losses, (d) a drink or drug problem or (e) illness at home;

- thwarted ambition and jealousy of colleagues;
- desire for a better standard of living;
- desire to 'beat the system', which may start off as a joke until its potential is realised.

RELATIONSHIPS

Security work generally involves regular contact with people and consequently is best undertaken in a relationship of goodwill and respect and in a friendly manner. In the process of building and maintaining this relationship, officers should never do or say anything that might later adversely affect the carrying out of their duties. The following examples reveal the danger:

- An officer obtained car engine parts gratis from a company's mechanic who listed them as being needed for a company vehicle. A thieving garage-hand caught by the officer threatened him into silence with this information.
- A gate officer who regularly accepted presents from a visiting contractor admitted this had stopped him taking action when he saw stolen property on the contractor's vehicle.
- An industrial tribunal adjudicating in a disciplinary matter lost all interest in the main issue when it was revealed that the officer had behaved aggressively and used obscene language. He was severely reprimanded.

It is not only to security that these considerations apply. It is a matter for conjecture as to how the reluctance of supervisors, managers and even company directors to take what is seen to be obvious action is explained by the fear that their own reprehensible behaviour may be exposed. Security professionals should never leave themselves vulnerable for the sake of some temporary benefit.

SUMMARY

Security work calls for integrity, common sense, confidence and sufficient knowledge of the legal aspects of the work to enable the security professional to avoid making mistakes. Performance will be enhanced by a smart appearance and deportment, alertness, good humour and patience, fairness and impartiality. Like all jobs it will have its moments of boredom, but these can be lightened if officers take an objective interest in the people around them.

2 General Security Duties

Security professionals should be in no doubt about what is expected of them. Their instructions should be written down to prevent any misunderstandings. In-house, these will take the form of the company rules applicable to all employees, supplemented by 'standing orders' or their equivalent that specifically relate to security duties. It is advisable for contract companies to provide comparable material for their employees. Obviously, spoken orders or briefings are adequate for routine matters arising during the ordinary working day, but where drills or plans have been agreed for emergencies, specific incidents or functions, these should be available for study by the security staff.

It is not possible to foresee all contingencies, and instructions should acknowledge that discretion may have to be exercised when the unexpected happens.

WORKS AND COMPANY RULES

Some works and company rules and standing orders are published on noticeboards and in handbooks, and may be available on computer through internal access media such as the intranet. Specific do's and don'ts may also be included in employment contracts. Any employee with security responsibilities must be thoroughly familiar with them, and in accordance with the policy of his employer, enforce them with tact and discretion.

ACCESS CONTROL

In its simplest form, access control refers to the measures taken to ensure that people and vehicles are only able to enter areas, buildings and rooms that they are legitimately entitled to enter, and at the times authorised.

Customers, suppliers, visitors and staff need a degree of access, but not to all areas. Some methods of exercising control can be almost prohibitively expensive no matter how desirable. A risk appraisal of the whole premises will show where effort should be concentrated. Areas such as research and development, the computer suite and product sales planning should have access restricted to those who work there, so electronically operated locks may be justified. These types of locks are activated by encoded magnetic keys or cards that can be personal to the user. Linked to a computer, this equipment can centrally record the comings and goings of the individual card user. Fixed closed-circuit television (CCTV) cameras can provide supplementary protection at entrances to high-risk areas.

Access control begins at the perimeter of the premises, which may be a fence, wall or shrubbery. A fence may incorporate electronic cabling in order to detect interference and may be linked to the operation of floodlighting and CCTV camera surveillance. Entry gates need to be substantial and, if needed, can have drop-arm barriers to control the flow and movement of traffic to the site. If a separate entrance is needed for pedestrians and there is a need to check them in, then it might be appropriate for the pedestrian entrance to incorporate turnstiles. On large sites, a gate office immediately next to a well-lit entrance is essential, with employee clocking points adjacent and clearly visible. At busy times, when individual identity cards cannot be checked, a person bypassing the clocking station would arouse suspicion. Identity cards with photographs can be coded so that holders can only enter high-security departments if they have authority to do so.

Between perimeter and buildings, a double fence, floodlighting, CCTV cameras, infra-red rays and other highly sophisticated equipment may be used to detect intruders.

The problems associated with internal car parking are best met by the issuing of personal employee car identification discs, which must be displayed in the parked vehicle, and by supervising entrances to the buildings where identification cards can be checked. During working hours, identification card colouring can be used to show immediately whether employees have the right to be where they are, and a similar coloured pass would indicate whether a visitor was straying from an authorised route. Out-of-hours access control could be provided by CCTV images on all sides of the building, coupled with internal intruder alarm systems and a security presence to respond to all incidents.

CALLERS

The first impression that visitors glean of an organisation is often from the approach and appearance of the security professional who greets them. When receiving callers the security professional must give the impression of being capable and efficient. Being smart in appearance and dealing with the visitor courteously are important in giving the visitor a good impression of the organisation. The caller's name and address should be recorded, together with the name of the person being visited. If the caller is expected, the person visited must be contacted and asked to attend to receive and escort the visitor. If this is not possible, someone – preferably another member of the security team – should be asked to escort the visitor to the correct destination. Once business has been completed, the time of departure of the visitor must be recorded.

'Walk-in thieves' often gain entry to premises by claiming to know a senior manager, hoping thereby that their bona fides will not be checked and that they will not require an escort. At night, ensure that the gatehouse door is kept locked. Instances are known of security officers being overcome by intruders after being drawn out of the gatehouse by some subterfuge. When alone, do not leave the building even at the request of a police officer in uniform unless you are completely satisfied as to his or her identity. If in doubt, telephone the local police station.

MUTUAL AID SCHEMES

Some companies and organisations run mutual aid schemes or business watches. These are set up to keep each other informed about crime, criminals and other security matters. This often takes the form of passing messages between member organisations using hand-held radio transmitters, paging systems or by using telephones. The police are prepared to get involved and may be the catalysts for setting up a new scheme. It is important that details of such a mutual aid scheme are kept confidential.

KEEPING RECORDS

Occurrence (log) book or computer database

Occurrence books are a useful tool when recording security duty information not recorded in other registers or in documents kept for a special purpose such as the search register. The occurrence book is an important record of all the activities of the security department and must be accurately compiled with the relevant details of all incidents. Slang terms must not be used, neither should alterations be made or text written between lines. Every entry that is made in the book should be signed by the person creating the entry, and the book should be read and initialled at the start of each duty.

If special pages are reserved for common occurrences, they must be used.

Search register or computer database

A search register should contain a record of every person and/or vehicle searched, including details of the date and time of the search, the works number and department of the person searched, the name of the security officer conducting the search, the location of the search and the reasons for it. In the case of a vehicle search, the registration number of the vehicle, its make and type should be noted, together with the details of the owner and driver. A search of the occupants should always be made when making a vehicle search. Searches cannot be conducted without consent (see Chapter 12).

A 'comment' column in the search register is valuable so that matters arising during the search can be noted. These might include any objections to the search, complaints about the conduct of the search or any other matter relevant to it. These comments may be important should an unsubstantiated allegation be made about harassment or the conduct of the search.

The search register should be kept conscientiously and retained, preferably, for a minimum of three years. If the police become involved in any incident arising out of a search, the search register will be evidence. Therefore it is important that accuracy is maintained.

Where records are kept on computer, access to the recorded information must be restricted to individuals who are authorised to view it. This might include the security manager, the director with responsibility for security and so on.

Lost and found property register or database

Employees must be satisfied that proper attention is paid to their claims that personal property has been lost or stolen, and therefore it is important that the details of losses and finds are recorded in the lost and found property register, or any computerised equivalent.

It is important to accurately describe lost and found property at the time of recording it, and that the description should include any identifying marks that will personalise it to the loser.

When money is handed to the security professional, whether on patrol or within any gatehouse or security office, the finder must be encouraged to count the money and then sign the entry in the property register (if handed in at the security point) or the officer's notebook (if handed to the officer when on patrol). If money is handed to an officer on patrol, it must be entered into the appropriate register or computer database at the earliest opportunity.

A label must be attached securely to any found property, and a number assigned to it that corresponds with the relevant entry in the register or computer database. The property should then be retained in a secure store or, in the case of money, a safe.

When property is claimed, the loser should sign for it in acknowledgement of its return. The finder should then be informed that the property has been returned to the loser.

There must be clear instructions for dealing with the disposal of unclaimed property, as it not only takes up valuable space but is a source of temptation. Retention for a period of one month is normally deemed adequate.

If there is any possibility that the reported property was lost outside the premises, the loser must be helped to report the facts to the local police. Property found outside the premises must not be accepted. Enquirers must be referred to the local police.

Motor vehicle register or database

An up-to-date record must be kept of employees who are owners of motor vehicles brought on to the premises. The record should include details of the make, type, colour and registration number of the vehicle, together with the name and works department details of the keeper. Such records will enable the keeper to be found in cases where the vehicle has to be moved quickly in an emergency, or where the vehicle is causing an obstruction or has been the subject of crime.

Key register or database

If keys of premises are kept in the care of the security department, care should be taken to ensure that they cannot be obtained by unauthorised persons. They must be kept in a locked cabinet and the cabinet key should be retained on the person of a member of the security staff while they are on duty. Insecure keys removed without authority may be used for an unlawful purpose and returned later unobserved. Only a person authorised to draw keys should be issued with them. Withdrawals and returns should be noted in a key register or computerised database. They must only be issued against the signature of the person requiring the keys.

Requests for keys at unusual times and without previous notice from an authorised person should be closely scrutinised and, if possible, the person wanting the key should be accompanied to the place concerned. Undue delay in returning keys must be investigated.

Vehicle log or database

A vehicle pass system is of dual value when goods are being delivered. This not only allows recorded entry into and egress from the premises, but provides for a signature to be entered by the recipient of the goods, who thereby acknowledges responsibility for acceptance.

Such records can serve many purposes. Some companies log the advice note numbers of all goods carried out in their vehicles, which forms a lasting record for easy reference. Where outside hauliers are concerned, the record facilitates checks on the numbers of journeys made where payment is involved, prevents a vehicle being locked inside the premises and may obviate complaints of unreasonable delay while vehicles have been waiting to be loaded or unloaded.

Telephone messages

The manner in which a telephone is answered can affect a caller's impression of a company. When calls are received after the office staff have gone home it is important to politely inform the caller that a message can be left and will be passed to the intended recipient as soon as possible. The caller should be asked whether the message is urgent or whether it can wait. The caller's name, address and telephone number should be noted, along with the time and date of the call and any brief message intended for the recipient. The information should be written on a memo and must include the details of the security officer or person taking the call (who, if asked by the caller, should provide their own name).

Where a caller is put through to an extension after hours, they must be told in advance if the extension has a voicemail facility. If the reception security officer has access to the e-mail address of the intended recipient of the call, a message containing a précis of the caller's enquiry should be sent.

GOOD HOUSEKEEPING

Staff sales

Where purchases of company property by employees are permitted, the employee should be in possession of some evidence of purchase or a sales receipt to show to security staff when leaving the premises. Arrangements are sometimes made for purchases to be taken to the security department for collection by employees when leaving work.

Sales receipts should be examined closely, and cancelled with a mark in order to prevent them being reused.

Suitcases and large parcels

Some organisations have rules designed to prevent employees from bringing large bags on to their premises. If an employee or visitor has acted in apparent ignorance of the rule, then the article should be retained (against a receipt) in the security office for collection when the employee leaves. However, this practice must be discouraged and the person reminded of the company rules. During times of high national security due to terrorism, the organisation might retain the right to search bags on entry, and refuse entry to those who do not give permission (see Chapter 12).

FIRST AID TREATMENT

Where a security officer is called upon to render first aid treatment to any person, a record must be made of the full details of that person, the nature of the occurrence causing the injury, the nature of the treatment given and any subsequent action taken.

The treatment of injured or ill people is best carried out by trained first aid personnel. If the security officer is not a certificated first aider then it is best to keep the casualty comfortable until trained assistance arrives. The carrying out of treatment by untrained personnel may cause significant harm to the casualty.

The preservation of the scene must be considered, especially where injury has resulted from a criminal or negligent act that might require the involvement of the police or the Health and Safety Executive. If a special form is in use for the reporting of accidents, this must be completed and forwarded for the attention of the company safety officer.

CONTRACTORS

No matter how frequently a contractor is engaged on the company premises, the contractor's employees have no constraints of loyalty as far as your company's property is concerned. Particularly in connection with building work, there may well be a floating population of workers employed for the duration of the contract.

Where there is a search clause in operation at the premises, that clause must be applied to all contractors as well as company employees. Searches should be made on a regular basis and it is recommended that one is carried out immediately the contract begins. In the course of patrolling, a watch should be kept on the scene of operations to ensure that workmen do not stray into prohibited areas. Contractors' vehicles should not be allowed to park near the site where they are working purely on the grounds of convenience; if contractors have tools to bring to the site, these should be dropped off where needed and the vehicles taken to a parking area where they offer no threat.

Officer's checklist in respect of contractors

- What are the conditions of the contract?
- Is a search clause included?

- Who is in charge of the contractor's workforce?

- Where and what is their job?

- Which items of the company's equipment are they allowed to use?

- Have any special safety instructions been given to the contractors and their workforce?

- Who is our company's liaison officer in respect of the work being done?

- What materials, if any, will be allowed to be taken off site?

- Where are the contractors' vehicles to be parked?

- Are there any subcontractors to be brought in? If so, will security be notified?

DISCIPLINARY MATTERS

With the exception of the offences of theft, criminal damage and contraventions of health and safety regulations, which will be dealt with in later chapters, the main disciplinary matters with which security professionals are likely to be involved are drunkenness, fighting, sleeping during working hours and, to a lesser extent, drugs misuse. Many companies seem reluctant to commit themselves to written policies about these matters, but some do have drug testing procedures. Any such incidents must be recorded and the details passed to senior management.

3 Patrolling Duties

When patrolling premises, the following are the main objectives:

- To prevent and detect fire.
- To prevent and detect any damage to company property and waste of company resources.
- To ensure company rules are observed.
- To prevent and detect offences against the company's interests and those of their employees – for example, theft or fraud.
- To prevent accidents or anything contrary to the company's obligations under health and safety at work regulations and the Fire Safety Order 2005 (see Chapter 18).

PATROLLING SECURITY OFFICERS

Duties will vary in accordance with the nature of the premises and the business that is being carried out there. Readers particularly concerned with site safety and fire patrols should refer to Chapters 17 and 18 respectively.

There are obvious problems for contract security staff if they are called upon to work in unfamiliar surroundings and at short notice. Unless a comprehensive briefing has been prepared for them, they will not know where to go, what to look for or what to do. The following checklist may be used:

- Check as soon as possible that all buildings, offices and working areas are secure and ensure that there is no fire, water leakage or other hazard.
- Ensure that all rooms and buildings left locked for security purposes are in order, with no interference to doors, padlocks, windows and fall-pipes. Padlocks must be carefully scrutinised to ensure they have not been interfered with or substituted.

- Check any rooms or building apparently left inadvertently unlocked. If there are no signs of interference with contents and there are no specific instructions to notify the occupiers, lock the door and make a note of the incident for bringing to the occupier's attention.

- Investigate all unusual lights and report the findings.

- Investigate all appliances that are left running. Do not turn them off unless there is no obvious reason for them being left on, or if they are likely to create an emergency such as overheating. Before turning off any appliance, verify that it has not been left on for a specific or intended purpose.

- Note any defects in the buildings that might result in damage or personal injury. Note missing roof slates, dangerous coping stones, holes in footpaths, loose stair treads and so on.

- Check perimeter fences and investigate any breaks that are found. Observe and note details of vehicles parked adjacent to the fence, or any items, such as cases and materials piled near to it, that may enable easy access and egress.

- Note matters that may affect employee welfare. For example, check vehicles in car parks whose lights have been left on, engines left running or tyres punctured. These should be reported to the owner where possible.

- Check seals on loaded vehicles, containers, railway vans and so on, to ensure there is no interference.

- Check commercial vehicles to ensure that they have been locked and immobilised. Details of insecure vehicles should be reported unless they have been parked within a locked building. Remove any key that may have been inadvertently left in the ignition or door locks of the vehicle, and report the matter accordingly.

- Note and report instances where materials subjected to weather damage have been left exposed.

- Pay special attention to loading bays and delivery areas where visiting drivers or internal transport may be operating. Investigate anything of a suspicious nature and report to your supervisor any activity that ceased abruptly on your appearance.

- Note and report any contravention of works rules to the supervisor of the person responsible and record the fact in the occurrence book or leave a report for your own supervisor.

- In the case of any hazard observed that may cause or produce an accident, take such steps that are necessary to remove the danger immediately.

- Investigate and challenge any person found on the premises whose presence you have any reason to regard as suspect. This should be done politely to avoid causing offence to a bona fide visitor.

- Where offences are observed at clocking stations, act in accordance with any instructions you have been given, and, in the absence of any such instructions, report the matter to your superiors. Do not take immediate action unless the instructions are to challenge suspected offenders forthwith.

- Pay special attention to safes, strong-rooms and cash offices where money may be available or perceived to be available. Where keys are found in locks, doors or drawers, these should be removed to a secure place.

- Outside normal working hours, visit areas where personnel are working to observe that no untoward activity is taking place.

- Report for early attention any defects in fencing, lighting, leaking taps, valves and so on.

- If the behaviour of any employees, visitors or others gives rise to the belief that they are using, or are in possession of drugs, report your suspicions to your superiors unless it is obvious that the person concerned needs medical treatment. Seize and report the finding of any article that has been apparently used to administer the drugs, and take care when handling such articles. (See Chapter 23 for more information.)

The above are examples of patrolling duties rather than an exhaustive list. Officers must be alert, interested and thorough. They must investigate anything that appears unusual, cultivate a suspicious mind, question anything about which there is the slightest doubt, get to know as much as possible about the manufacturing and other processes in which the company is involved and as much about the company's documentation as necessary. They must learn the identities of the people in charge of departments so as to be able to communicate with them with confidence and with knowledge of the work for which they are responsible.

Frequency of patrols

Many factors influence the frequency of a patrol, including the length and complexity, as well as vulnerability to one or more of the risks that patrolling is designed to combat. Patrols should be conducted irregularly so that the security officer's arrival at any one point cannot be anticipated. To prevent any interested party estimating where the patrol will be, it is sometimes best to retrace steps from time to time and to vary the route of the patrol.

Use of vehicles in patrolling

On a large, dispersed site, radio-equipped transport is a time-saving necessity. It also enables contract security companies to offer clients out-of-hours spot visiting at several sites. A fixed visiting routine is clearly undesirable because potential intruders observing from a safe distance would soon become aware of the amount of time at their disposal between security checks.

While the nature of the premises may allow subsequent checks to be purely visual, the initial check should be thorough. If the vehicle has to be left unattended it must be locked and immobilised; the loss of a vehicle would not advance the company's security reputation! If any suspicion is raised by the unusual presence of a car nearby, glimpses of figures in the darkness or simply a 'gut' feeling, before a routine inspection is carried out the officer must inform control. If, for example, a car is parked outside a building, block it in with the patrol vehicle and investigate. It is the judgement of the patrolling officer that will determine whether the police should be contacted.

All visits should be scrupulously recorded if no clocking system is used. It is a common complaint of clients that agreed visits are not made. If a visit is not made, the reason for this should be logged in case an explanation is required.

Patrolling building sites

Careless disregard of good housekeeping principles leads to wastage and an unwarranted assumption of theft on building sites. Lack of interest in the safe storage of tools and materials causes temptation and subsequent loss that could be avoided if senior personnel were alerted to particular instances.

Where security duties include the patrolling of any site where building operations are in progress, the following points should be observed and reported on:

- Pipes, boilers, radiators, electrical and other equipment left in unlocked buildings or huts or clearly in public view.

- Braziers and electric fires left burning among wooden buildings or stacked timber, and any plant unnecessarily left running.

- Cement bags stacked in the open, exposed to moisture and the elements, or concrete mixers left with their wheels embedded in hardening concrete.

- Windows and door frames stacked loosely at the roadside and subject to damage.

- Lavatory suites, wash basins, baths and so on left in the open and likely to become exposed to damage and theft.

- Signs of careless usage of materials and resultant damage by workers such as cartons of nails strewn about, plaster mixed on newly laid floor boarding and bundles of wires dropped in mud.

- Off-cuts of metals such as plumbing piping, aluminium conduit and fittings of all types, left where there is a possibility of theft.

- Wastage of water by taps left running or leakage from unfinished or damaged piping.

- Unlit and dangerous obstructions left on roads, any warning lamps missing or broken.

- Signs of someone sleeping out in buildings.

- Vehicles left for no obvious reason on the site, or vehicles seen cruising around. In such a case the vehicle details should be noted and, where possible, the driver questioned.

The following recommendations are offered:

- Watch paths of houses adjoining the area for new bricks, kerbstones and flagging of the type being used on the building site.

- Pay special attention to the unloading of materials for site use to ensure no opportunity arises for part to remain on the delivering vehicles for removal to the driver's advantage.

- Observe the locality and report details of any rubble such as old bricks and stones that could be used as missiles to cause damage to the new properties.

- Watch what employees take to their vehicles at finishing time and query anything suspicious.

- Report on any safety or fire hazards that have been observed. Also, report any security weaknesses that have been identified.

There are aids available to make for a more efficient and proficient patrol. Some may need to be implemented on the initiative of the security officer. For example:

- Use a guard dog if you are trained in their use and capable of controlling one, provided there are no managerial objections.

- Ask for guard dog warning notices to be displayed around the site, whether there is a dog on site or a dog patrol. (If a dog is used these are required by law.)

- Ask for 'Reward for information concerning damage' notices to be displayed around the site.

- Vary patrols and visiting times as much as possible.

- Ask for lighting to be provided for compounded areas and to be left on during the hours of darkness.

On outlying building sites the security officer may be more exposed to the weather and the danger of attack. Therefore:

- Have adequate clothing available for all conditions, especially strong boots and waterproof clothing.

- Carry a robust torch and communications to raise the alarm if necessary.

- Arrange some form of regular communication with other security officers so that early alarm can be raised in the event of an emergency or personal attack.

- Do not become exposed to needless risk where several intruders are involved. Get assistance.

KEY CARRYING

If patrol duties necessitate the possession of keys in quantity, as may happen in shopping precincts for example, ensure that they are firmly attached to the body and, if possible, are not easy to get at and not clearly visible. If keys are stolen or lost, lock replacement has to be immediate and is likely to incur considerable cost to the company.

COMMUNICATIONS

Where there is a particularly large area to patrol it will probably be divided into numbered sectors, similar to the beat areas used by the police.

When commencing a patrol it is important to tell a security colleague or perhaps a night supervisor which sector you are going to patrol and the time that you are expected to return to the security point. If there is no other security officer on the premises, it is advisable to leave a note in a register indicating where you are likely to be and the time of your return. If there is an officer at a base, it is important that regular calls are made to that officer as an initial safety precaution.

If the site is equipped with radio communications for radio contact, it must be borne in mind that one of the conditions of the operating licence is that correct procedure is used by callers. A formal system must be used that keeps conversation to a minimum and that discourages casual conversation. It should also be remembered that wavebands overlap and, as a consequence, what is said may be heard by others. If in doubt about the content or context of a message, ask for it to be repeated.

Radio equipment is a costly commodity and should be looked after. It must not be dropped. It is best attached to clothing at all times, and ready-made harnesses are available for this purpose. Radio equipment should be carried quite openly so that it will be seen that the officer has the means to communicate information and can obtain assistance should the need arise. Anything of a confidential nature must not be transmitted within the hearing of bystanders.

Radio transmission technique

The two essentials of good radio transmission technique are brevity and clarity, which are enhanced by the use of recognised abbreviations and use of the phonetic alphabet. Time references should always use the 24-hour clock.

A code word or call-sign must be allocated to the base station and individual call-signs given to each officer. At the start of duty each officer must log on to their radio indicating whether the signal is clear or weak. Battery charge levels should be checked before use.

Phonetic alphabet

A Alpha	**H** Hotel	**O** Oscar	**V** Victor
B Bravo	**I** India	**P** Papa	**W** Whiskey
C Charlie	**J** Juliet	**Q** Quebec	**X** X-ray
D Delta	**K** Kilo	**R** Romeo	**Y** Yankee
E Echo	**L** Lima	**S** Sierra	**Z** Zulu
F Foxtrot	**M** Mike	**T** Tango	
G Golf	**N** November	**U** Uniform	

Recognised terms and abbreviations

There are a number of different terms and abbreviations in use. None is exclusively better than any other. However, it is important that the set of abbreviations and terms used are the ones used by all on the site. The terms and abbreviations used must be agreed as a matter of security policy. Some of the abbreviations might include:

Over	End of this transmission to you. I expect a reply.
Out	End of my transmission. I do not expect a reply.
Roger	Message received and understood.
Wilco	Message received, understood and will be acted upon.
Repeat	Message not clearly understood or received. Please repeat.
Standby	Not able or ready to give an immediate reply.
ETA	Estimated time of arrival.
ETD	Estimated time of departure.

When transmitting, speech must be clear and steady and rather slower than normal. A raised voice, perhaps in irritation at bad reception, may cause distortion in the signal. Messages must be kept business like and short, using simple language that can be clearly understood and not misinterpreted. Joking and gossiping must be avoided when 'on air'.

INTRUDERS

Security personnel are in the front line when it comes to the defence of an employer's interests, so it is as well to remember that in some cases there is a risk of bodily injury from intruders. When dealing with intruders it is best to get help and not deal with them single-handedly, particularly if they are suspected of being in possession of a dangerous weapon. A security officer who can identify intruders by offering a good description and details of their escape route and any vehicle used is more useful than an unconscious one who is unable to recognise their attacker.

The amount of force a security officer may use against offenders or suspected offenders is that which is reasonably necessary to arrest or prevent the escape of the person (this will be more fully explained in Chapter 10). Trespassers who have not committed an offence but who refuse to leave premises when requested to do so may be ejected using reasonable force (see 'Trespass' in Chapter 9).

VULNERABLE PLACES

When visiting warehouses, stores and offices where there is a high risk of loss by theft, take care not to give notice of approach by heavy footsteps or the flashing of a torch. If there appears to be something wrong with the premises being inspected, colleagues must be warned and assistance mustered before a search is made.

If there are obvious signs of entry and a possibility that intruders are still inside, assistance must be obtained and the police notified. A watch must be kept on the premises and entry must not be made until the police arrive. When searching a large building, especially an office block, switch lights on as you go and, where possible, lock off sections that have already been searched. Where premises contain a known danger to personnel, as in the case of a garage pit, lights must be turned on before entry is made.

PROPERTY FOUND IN SUSPICIOUS CIRCUMSTANCES

It is common practice for a thieving employee to hide property that has been stolen from an employer on the premises or close to the perimeter fence for later removal. Should the security officer come across anything which, from its nature and the place where it has been discovered, causes suspicion that it may have been stolen, it should not initially be moved. Observations should be kept on the property from a safe distance so that the person returning to retrieve it can be identified.

Anyone seen removing the property should be allowed to do so and followed until the opportunity arises for apprehension in the presence of a member of the managerial or supervisory staff or another member of the security staff. Once apprehended, the person must be given the opportunity to explain their possession of the property and, if the explanation indicates that the property is or may be stolen, the policy of the employer must be followed.

Property found outside the perimeter can similarly be observed. If there is a likelihood that the property will be removed to the detriment of the employer, then an arrest may be made if there are reasonable grounds for believing the person to be in the act of stealing, which is an indictable offence. Once the suspect has been detained, the police should be called. A time limit must be put on observations. If the workforce in general becomes aware that security are engaged in observation, the operation must be discontinued immediately and the property recovered.

Any property found by patrols that is suspicious or is believed to have been used by intruders in the commission of a crime must be seized and removed to a safe place. Care must be taken when handling the articles as they may provide forensic or fingerprint evidence that will assist in the detection of the crime.

The finding of such property, implements or articles must be logged in the security officer's notebook and in the occurrence book. The information recorded should include the time, date, place and location of the find as well as a full description of the property. If the property does prove to have been stolen, the security officer may need to give a written statement to the police that will include the circumstances of its finding and recovery.

WEARING A UNIFORM

Section 52(2) of the Police Act 1964 prohibits any person other than a member of the civil police from wearing any article of uniform in circumstances where it gives an appearance so resembling the uniform of a member of the police force as to be calculated to deceive others. *Intent* to deceive is not a necessary part of the evidence required to obtain a successful prosecution. The section was introduced to control the wearing in public places of uniforms similar to police uniforms.

Remember at all times that wearing a uniform makes a strong impression on an observer and can determine whether the security officer is regarded with respect or otherwise. The uniform must be kept clean and as neat as possible.

SECURITY PERSONNEL CARRYING WEAPONS

The routine carrying of a weapon, or as part of the uniform, should be discouraged. While it is an offence to possess any article made, intended or adapted for use as an offensive weapon (Prevention of Crime Act 1953) in a public place, this does not extend to private property, which includes places of work, provided that the public do not have general access by payment or other means.

AMATEUR AND PROFESSIONAL THIEVES

In the course of patrolling or guarding premises with high-value contents, the security officer must not disregard what is happening outside the site. Any unusual and lengthy interest shown in premises by persons in a vehicle or loitering in the street should be noted by recording vehicle registration numbers and descriptions. If the circumstances are repeated, there are definite grounds for suspicion and this must be reported to other security staff and the police. Well-organised thieves carefully plan their operations and select targets on the following principles:

- the value of the target as against the likely risk;
- the accessibility of the target and whether it is transportable or easily disposed of;
- the opportunity to plan and assess the likelihood of success;
- the ease of access and whether the site is observed;
- adequate and uninterrupted time to carry out the project;
- a ready means of quick escape, not involving the use of violence;
- the relative certainty of remaining undetected.

Some thieves are more unpredictable and may act spontaneously. Some may be under the influence of drink or drugs, which will affect rationality and may make them more dangerous. Such thieves may:

- select target premises purely on the grounds of vulnerability rather then knowledge of the contents;
- take greater risks with regards to noise and damage during exit and entry;

- have little regard for the presence of security or other staff working on the premises;
- cause senseless internal damage;
- steal indiscriminately;
- act totally unpredictably if challenged by security or other staff working on the premises.

Patrolling is an integral part of the security officer's duties. It must not be taken lightly because it plays a key role in community safety, the prevention of crime and the protection of an organisation's assets.

4

Security in Public Places

Private and contract security personnel are increasingly employed on duties that bring them into constant contact with the general public, often in crowded and relatively small areas. To some extent this is a consequence of the growth of shopping precincts, but it also follows the increase in some categories of property crime that has necessitated additional precautions in all the larger retail establishments and hotels, and their diversification to unlikely targets such as hospitals and universities.

There is one feature common to these work areas that does not apply to employee-orientated in-company security practice. There is no industrial relations breach of discipline safety net to justify unwise security action when members of the public are affected. The consequences may be, at the least, complaints and bad publicity extending to possible civil action to the detriment not just of the offending officer but also of his employer, and, where contract security is in use, possibly even the client. It follows that those expected to work satisfactorily in such environments must have adequate knowledge of their objectives, the legal powers they have at their disposal, the constraints they have to observe and the public relations factors they should bear in mind. All this can only be achieved by training, and by having detailed instructions to which to refer. Contract companies must not allow expediency to persuade them to put an inexperienced officer on such a job, unless accompanied by a competent partner, because doing so could damage the security company's reputation.

It is arguable that none of the places mentioned is strictly 'public'; hotels certainly are not, because the public do not have unrestricted access, but as with most incorporate restaurant facilities a semblance of respectability will permit unchallenged entry, with the potential then to stray further. All, however, share similarities and problems that differentiate them from the more traditional scenes of security activity.

SHOPPING PRECINCTS

A security force should be competent to cope with minor matters and have the organisational back-up to deal with lost and found property, missing children, accidents, general first aid and petty disturbances that can be stopped short of violence. On the other hand, its members should have the capability and confidence to act immediately if a more serious matter such as robbery, burglary, serious assault, criminal damage or theft takes place in their presence, or, if reported to them, sense enough to take the initial steps needed pending police arrival, such as ensuring the safety of the complainant, protecting the crime scene and collecting details of witnesses.

A smart appearance and deportment convey an impression of authority and efficiency to the public whose respect is essential if acceptance and cooperation is to be acquired. Care should be taken so as not to spoil that image by resorting to prolonged casual gossiping with members of the public or openly relaxing inside shops with an obvious indifference to what is going on outside. The open carrying of large bunches of keys almost seems to be a status symbol for precinct officers. This should be discouraged and will have serious implications for management if they are lost or stolen.

Radio transceivers connected to a central control room are essential for patrolling a well-run precinct. The radio handsets should be carried quite openly, symbolising a team with modern communications that can obtain immediate back-up in an emergency. An officer sensibly positioned near the site of an incipient disturbance may find that the use of the transceiver in an obvious manner induces second thoughts on the part of troublemakers. Adherence to official procedure when transmitting calls reinforces this image as close passers-by will hear some of what is said, although this point should be remembered when any form of sensitive message is to be sent.

Any officer with a recognised first aid qualification will be a great asset, together with that officer's knowledge of the first aid facilities available within the precinct. There is little more incongruous than the sight of a uniformed officer standing helplessly while someone else tries to help a sick or injured person. Similarly, and even more so in the case of fire, there must be familiarity with the positioning and types of equipment and the procedures to be followed. A feature of patrolling must be to ensure that avenues specified for use by fire tenders and appliances are not obstructed, and that fixed fire-fighting installations and equipment are not obstructed and are operational. Safety factors must not be overlooked. Items like broken gratings, drain covers, gully grates, vandalised seats or telephone kiosks should all be noted and reported for action. In fact, anything that could cause harm to tenants or users of the precinct, including malpractice by tenants, should be reported.

Drug abuse, begging, and male and female importuning will all embarrass and alienate customers. The symptoms and indications of addicts should be recognised (see Chapter 23). Those soliciting or begging will, in all probability, remove themselves as soon as approached. Homosexual activity in toilets can be discouraged by frequent but irregular visits in the course of patrolling.

Theft from shops will inevitably be encountered. Precinct management must recognise this and should have formulated procedures for action. A patrolling officer must know these procedures and know of the 'private person' powers of arrest. For this and any other type of offence a priority for the security officer is to note details of witnesses from whom statements may be taken. If, during evening patrols, premises are found to be broken into, assistance should be sought before making entry into the insecure premises. If entry is made, the officer must disturb very little if anything at all, because this may hinder the police specialist who may wish to examine the area for evidence left by an intruder. Burglar alarms, smoke and dye emitting systems, and fire alarms will be widely, if not universally installed, and their type and whereabouts should be noted. Some shopping precincts have 'Shop Alert' systems that are a means of communicating details of certain messages or warnings to other such systems and any security control room.

The security officer should check premises within the precinct as soon as they have been vacated and any sign of insecurity, such as lights left on or any other concerns of an unusual nature, should be notified to the control room so that a keyholder can be called out. A further contingency that management should take into consideration is evacuation in the event of bomb threats or other emergencies. In such cases the actions of security officers should be spelled out to them (Chapter 19 contains more information). As always, a good working relationship with local police patrols can be a great help.

Patience, good humour, helpfulness and smartness all contribute in building up a good relationship with patrons. It is interesting to watch and speculate about people en masse; by doing this, observation is improved and suspect types more easily identified.

Pickpockets

Periodic incursions may be made by pickpockets, either singly or as a team. The favourite operating conditions for pickpockets is when saturation shopping is taking place, such as at Christmas or on public holidays, or when the precinct is crowded for a special occasion and patrons' attention is diverted by, say, a shop opening by a celebrity or a major sale. Visiting football fans may create the requisite congestion and diversion. Amateurs will concentrate on purses on view in the tops of bags, but professionals are much more difficult to spot. Neither is likely to operate in the sight of a uniform. Professionals select a victim, then push or barge them so that they may be more concerned with the affront to their dignity than with what is going on. Stolen items are always got rid of as soon as possible – in a team, to another member. Where the officer spots pickpockets, the offenders should be observed until security assistance or the police arrive. Also, the victim's details must be obtained so that they can be passed on to the police.

Shops and supermarkets

Theft in retail premises affects the profitability of the operation; in some cases shops have ceased trading because of so-called 'shrinkage'. In any event, most retail operations have fixed costs such as the cost of goods to be displayed for sale, the lease of the premises, lighting, heating, local authority rates and so on. These costs may vary only a little over time. In some cases, the only flexible cost that management has is that of the number of staff employed and, if losses from retail premises become excessive and threaten profitability, management may have to release staff. It therefore goes without saying that the responsibility for reducing loss in retail premises falls on every employee, not just on security staff.

Security in shops and supermarkets has, until recently, been focused on store detectives, occasionally supplemented by out-of-hours guarding. Now, uniformed personnel are increasingly being placed on the shopfloor among patrons as a deterrent not just to stealing but also to rowdy behaviour. Akin to this is the rare, dangerous practice known as 'steaming'. Steaming is an organised form of gang stealing perpetrated mostly in busy city centres and occasionally in shopping precincts. Its *modus operandi* is that of a gang of youths suddenly appearing among packed shoppers, racing through them, knocking people aside, snatching handbags and taking whatever can be taken from counters. Some are apt to carry weapons and do not hesitate to use violence. If a build-up of these suspect types is noted in shop entrances there should be no delay in warning the police; no harm is done if the fears prove unfounded.

The security professional must maintain a smart, alert appearance and must know the location of every counter, department or service within the premises. What special skills are required will depend on whether first aid or fire-trained staff are employed for those specific purposes, but as in precinct security, the officer must be competent. The areas of maximum effectiveness of presence should be those where losses are known to be the greatest and in the vicinity of, or exits leading to, stockrooms, staff cloakrooms and lockers, and entrances most likely to be used by troublemakers, such as those near to public houses and the like. Flexibility of movement will of course be at management discretion, but attention should be paid to loading bays when in use. It must not be forgotten that a substantial amount of loss is perpetrated by employees.

Extra vigilance is called for when cash is moved internally or is transported from or into premises. Immediate assistance should be rendered to store detectives when necessary, as violence is increasingly being used by offenders in order to prevent legitimate arrest.

Store detectives must be trained in their legal powers of arrest and the use of force, as outlined in Chapter 10. If they exceed these powers or take action that is unjustified, both they and their employers may be open to civil action for damages (and the accompanying bad publicity). Careful observation must be made to establish the facts, followed by legally correct action carried out firmly but as unobtrusively as possible, with minimum embarrassment to the suspect.

Questioning and conversation should be kept on a non-aggressive and non-recriminatory level, with as much display of good-natured understanding as the circumstances permit. If a genuine mistake has been made, the fact that a store detective has acted reasonably will be a mitigating factor. The person making the arrest thereby assumes some responsibility for the detained person's well-being; the guidance on searching discussed in Chapter 12 should always be borne in mind. If the detained suspect is awkward and there are grounds for suspecting possession of other stolen property, he or she must be kept under observation at all times until the police arrive. If possible, the personal details of the detained person should be noted, including name, date of birth and address. If these are refused, the refusal should be notified to the police when they attend and this should be done in the presence of the detained person, so that when given on demand to the police officer they can be noted.

When making an arrest, the presence of a fellow employee acting as a witness has dual value, evidentially and as a deterrent against escape. If the locality is one where there have been incidents in which store detectives have been assaulted by accomplices, it is clearly advisable to have extra assistance on hand. There is legally no need to delay an arrest until the suspect has passed the final payment point, but in many cases it will be better to allow this in order to rebut a defence that the suspect intended to pay and was not given the opportunity to do so. Companies may have their own instructions on the policy to be followed.

It is the responsibility of the police to provide evidence to prove the offence, questioning the suspect and obtaining statements from witnesses. Therefore, no questioning of the suspect should be carried out by the security officer or store detective at this time. Any relevant conversation such as an admission of the offence should be noted and relayed to the police in the presence of the suspect.

Ruses used by shoplifters are many and varied. The most common is to put stolen property into pockets or bags. Others include the following:

- false bottoms in shopping bags;
- poacher pockets sewn into clothing;
- opening hollow objects that are to be purchased genuinely and placing items inside;
- putting goods into rolled-up umbrellas or newspapers;
- pushing goods down into high boots;
- false pregnancy;
- placing items in or under headgear;
- leaving changing rooms with clothing underneath normal clothing;
- price-ticket swapping.

In addition, in order to beat electronic tagging systems, some shoplifters resort to lining shopping bags with tinfoil. A view of this in shopping bags may well indicate the presence of a shoplifter. Also, watch has to be kept for diversionary incidents such as quarrels, apparent fainting or illness, or disturbances among groups of people. Attention should then be paid to counters containing high-value goods that are outside the immediate area. Thieves may operate singly, in which case the person will probably stand looking around before acting, or as a team, in which case the actual thief will concentrate on stealing goods and be given 'cover' by the others.

After an arrest is made, care should be taken while escorting the detained person to make sure nothing is disposed of. As in precinct security another species of criminal may be encountered – the pickpocket – whose presence, while not affecting the profitability of the shop, will harm its reputation.

Store detectives may regularly be called upon to give evidence in court and must therefore be punctilious in the use of their notebooks. They should be capable of writing their own evidence statements, and both competent and confident at giving evidence in court. New recruits ought to be given a period of court attendance during their training. The work of the store detective will often be concerned with employees, and it is therefore necessary that they know their company's disciplinary codes and procedures. Particular areas where employee malpractice may be encountered are delivery and dispatch bays, withdrawals from stockrooms, employee discount purchasing and till frauds, including collusion in sales to friends, relatives and fellow staff. Where searching is an accepted condition of employment, this should be carried out regularly and conscientiously and with regard to the Chapter 12 guidelines on searching.

HOSPITALS

The nature of a hospital gives rise to a unique range of problems. These include:

- For a large part of the day the public have virtually unrestricted access to the site.

- There is constant legitimate activity throughout the day and night using numerous entry points to buildings.

- The nature of some ancillary work is such that it does not attract a high calibre of employee and there are ample opportunities for petty pilfering.

- In some jobs – for example, that of a porter – there is an unquestioned right to be almost anywhere within the premises.

- The premises hold a wide range of targets of value, including drugs, consumable medical supplies, linen, clothing, cash, food, and office and technical equipment.

- The presence of nurses and their residences may well attract persons inclined towards indecent exposure or the commission of other sex offences.

- A high volume of vehicles parked on-site may lead to an increase in vehicle crime.

- The presence of injured and drunk or drugged individuals in accident and emergency departments may lead to assaults on staff.

- Security may not be given a high priority.

- The possible abduction of newly born infants.

In addition to all these is the threat of havoc that could be caused by fire or some other disaster. Fire authorities will have detailed plans for such eventualities, and a security priority must be to keep access routes clear of obstruction for incoming emergency service vehicles. This will also mean strict enforcement of parking restrictions, which at some times of day may constitute the most time-consuming part of patrolling.

Internal theft enquiries will almost certainly be the responsibility of the head of the security department. In many hospitals this individual is the only security presence, and they generally have an advisory role and a roving commission, aiming to achieve the highest degree of security possible within the constraints imposed by management. The head of security will have to become familiar with existing plans in relation to emergencies like fire, flooding or other natural or installation disasters, and will make improvement recommendations where possible. However, the main task of this individual will be the reduction of theft, fraud, damage and assault. A simple system of recording and reporting incidents is needed in order to pinpoint problem areas and possible suspects. A survey and assessment of risk will also be needed, requiring discussion with senior executives, providing an opportunity for establishing personal contacts, brain-picking and indoctrination. Including a practical talk on security in staff induction training is useful if it is focused on hospital problems and made interesting by quoting examples. If not already established, a means of identification for staff and their cars should be advocated as this will help in the control of unauthorised entry on to the site and parking enforcement.

A physical check will show where lighting can be improved, where better locks can be fitted (especially in sensitive areas such as pharmacies, computer suites and laboratories), where non-essential doors can be turned into fire doors and where compounds can be erected around external fuel tanks, gas storage and electricity sub-stations for safety purposes. Well-advertised CCTV systems with video recording could both deter criminals and provide evidence for the accident and emergency situations involving violence that are motivating demands for better security. Camera coverage could be extended to other parts of the hospital, thus minimising personnel requirements. The head of security must not overlook the fact that hospitals are consumers and are no more immune to corrupt practices than other organisations. The opportunities for theft by the workforce are legion, and simple changes in handling procedures may reduce the scope for crime.

The duties of other hospital security personnel will vary according to the location and nature of the premises. Buildings set in country surroundings are not comparable to those in built-up areas. The controlling management of hospitals may have divergent views, influenced by recent incidents and possibly by union reaction to them. Also, finance will be an overriding consideration, and those who are employed in security must be philosophical in accepting a judge's comment – 'that a precaution is physically possible does not mean it is reasonably practicable'.

The exclusion of the undesirable, the unauthorised and the ill-intentioned is clearly facilitated by personal identification badges. In the absence of these it will be much more difficult to identify suspect persons, and when suspects are challenged, instinct might dictate that the person should be accompanied to where they claim to be going. Someone who is untruthful will be a trespasser at the least, and should be treated accordingly. Accident and emergency departments should be patrolled by the security officer at identified risk times, such as at the end of licensing hours, as should the walkways to nurses' residences after dark. All the usual factors in patrolling will apply, including a good knowledge of the site. With a largely youthful female workforce, security staff must not develop casual relationships that could affect the performance of their duties or bring them into disrepute.

HOTELS

Hotel security incorporates an assortment of the problems mentioned in the previous sections. Some personnel in hotels are low paid and therefore there is likely to be a large staff turnover with, in many instances, inadequate vetting of applicants. Theft by employees is therefore to be expected where their work gives them unrestricted access to all areas of the hotel, including guest rooms. Hotel bars and lounges are happy hunting grounds for prostitutes, offering an immediate supply of wealthy clients with comfortable accommodation available. A clear statement is needed by management on the policy to be followed, which should cover disciplinary action against employees acting as touts or procurers. Prostitutes stick to pitches and may soon become known to security. Guest drug users are again a matter on which management will want the final say, but management must refer traffickers to the police for arrest.

Theft of food can be a persistent source of loss in hotels. This type of theft is not always confined to kitchen staff and is often difficult to identify. It can take the form of acceptance of short deliveries, corruption between buyer and supplier, excess withdrawals from stores, or outright theft from stores or from the kitchen itself. The cultivation of a 'well-wisher' or recruitment of an undercover agent on to the staff can be an invaluable aid in identifying suspects. Siting the till where it can be clearly seen so that it can be read by customers will help to cut bar losses, but identifying overcharging by a waiter service will require customer complaint and may only be possible with the help of outsiders making test purchases. The approximate percentage of bar profits should be known and, if there is any significant variation from what is expected, this should be investigated. A water-tight system of transfer of cash from bar and restaurant tills to the cashier's safe should be enforced. Actual and fake robberies are not unknown, and wages are still sometimes paid in cash. In this respect, all the usual precautions should be implemented.

Some guests will inevitably indulge in 'souvenir'-type theft of coat-hangers, towels, ash trays and other items management would not wish to pursue. However, many hotels now affix the hotel's name to anything portable. It is theft from guests that can hurt the hotel the most, and hotels cannot avoid liability simply by posting disclaimer notices around the premises, although liability may be limited, especially if a client does not lodge valuables in the hotel safe. All losses must be recorded, and the more serious ones, where the loser insists, should be reported to the police. Data can then be drawn up that may identify a pattern indicating that a certain person is involved, thus facilitating an operation to apprehend the offender. Where a key is lost it should be considered stolen and the lock changed or, where doors are operated on a card access system, the card access code withdrawn.

Credit card and cheque frauds are frequent, but strict adherence to checking procedures should keep these within bounds. Some companies give a reward for anyone spotting a stolen credit card. CCTV in the reception area with video recording is recommended, with additional cameras sited at other exits and entries, delivery doors and car parking areas. The control of people will be greatly enhanced if employees are issued with identity badges, which, when they leave employment, should be surrendered.

Hotel security is still primarily a matter for a plain-clothes security manager or officer who, with time and experience, will develop the instinct that tells them when something is wrong with an apparently respectable individual. This person must ensure that their responsibilities are recognised by all managers and that reasonable cooperation is forthcoming. It goes without saying, also, that the security team must have a good working relationship with the local police.

Sudden deaths do occur in hotels and a set drill for dealing with them should be established. Where there is a death on the premises, the room involved must be locked and nothing disturbed until the police arrive. In any event, a sudden death must be reported to the police who will act on behalf of the coroner. Possessions of the deceased must be carefully listed in the presence of another person and put in a sealed container pending disposal to a next of kin. The police will offer guidance in this respect.

Where uniformed personnel are used, their role will be similar to their counterparts in retail premises. Efforts should be concentrated in reception areas, car parks, the vicinity of lifts and in the night patrolling of floors, with fire prevention being a priority.

SMOKING IN PUBLIC PLACES

The Health Act 2006, makes it an offence to smoke in a smoke-free place. Smoke-free places are premises that are used as a place of work, or where members of the public attend for the purpose of receiving goods or services from the person or persons working there

It is the duty of any person who controls or who is concerned in the management of smoke-free premises to cause a person there to stop smoking – a person who fails to comply with this duty commits an offence. It is clear that the security professional will be a person who is concerned in the management of smoke-free premises and as such should request anyone who is smoking to stop immediately. If the request to stop smoking has been made, then the defence that reasonable steps were taken to cause a person that is smoking to stop may be applicable.

The ban covers: tobacco, cigarettes, pipes, cigars and herbal tobacco. These products become prohibited the moment they are lit, even if the person is not smoking them at the time.

5   Cash Security

Duties in respect of the safekeeping of a company's money fall into several categories:

- collection of wages or petty cash from a bank by company personnel and vehicles;
- the banking of cash using company personnel and vehicles;
- supervision during collection of cash for banking by commercial carriers;
- reception of wages from commercial cash carriers;
- guarding of wages during packet make-up and pending payout;
- providing a security presence during payout;
- inspection of safes, strongrooms and cashiers' offices outside of normal working hours.

A person in charge of security may well have additional auditor-type responsibility in the checking of petty cash vouchers, procedures, cheque handling and safekeeping and so on.

MOVEMENT OF MONEY BY COMPANY STAFF

If a company insures its cash, the method and means of holding and moving money must have the insurer's approval. This is particularly important for the collection and delivery of substantial funds; strict limitations are likely to be imposed on the maximum sums that can be carried by company personnel without the use of commercial carriers (whose own insurance would provide cover during the period which was formerly of maximum danger – transit between bank and customer). On purely financial grounds it may be advantageous to use a specialist company, thus minimising risks to employees.

When handling or transporting cash, the security officer must always wear any protective equipment provided, and, in the face of any personal attack there should be no heroics – a seriously injured security officer is a cost no employer is prepared to pay for the safety of money.

Movement on foot

The transportation of money on foot is asking for trouble, even when relatively small sums are being carried. The practice must not be considered if there is a conceivable alternative. However, the following advice is tendered:

- A minimum of two people should be used. Preferably, both male and both physically fit.

- Temporary or casual staff must not be used to transport cash.

- The use of a bag may present an opportunity for a quick grab. It may be better to disperse notes in pockets or within a cash carrying garment, such as a waistcoat, with coins only in a bag.

- If a bag is used, some are available that are designed solely for the carrying of cash. These incorporate audible alarms and emit a smoke or dye that will render the banknotes useless other than to banks. The bag should be carried by an able-bodied person.

- Bags must never be chained to a wrist or other parts of the body, unless with an easily broken connection that activates an in-built protective device within the bag.

- Before setting off, inform the bank. Make arrangements with them that will avoid the need to wait in queue on arrival.

- Short cuts via side streets must be avoided. The carrier must keep to busy streets, walking purposefully, away from the kerb edge and, when possible, on the side of the road facing oncoming traffic. At night, carriers should stick to well-lit routes.

- The escort should walk marginally behind the carrier, keeping an eye out for any suspicious activity. If something suspicious is noted the cash carrier must be escorted to a place of safety or to a location where there are plenty of other people.

- The entrance to a bank is a danger area. Pausing at the doorway is a good idea as it gives officers an opportunity to spot potential assailants.

- Times and routes must be varied as much as possible, particularly where the transportation of cash on foot is a regular occurrence.

Movement by vehicle

When moving cash by vehicle, the danger period is when crossing the pavement to and from the bank. An attack on the vehicle itself is much less likely, unless the amount of cash being carried justifies a well-planned and reconnoitred operation. If a large amount of cash is being carried, the insurers will have insisted on modifications to a vehicle at least to the extent of the following:

- providing means of securing the cash carrying box or bag firmly to the chassis of the vehicle using eye bolts or a chain;
- welding a special box to the chassis of the vehicle;
- strengthening and making all doors lockable from the inside;
- fitting double locks to all doors to ensure that they cannot be opened once a window has been smashed;
- fitting an audible alarm, with a personal attack option, operated by an internal switch;
- fitting a two-way radio or mobile phone with a pre-programmed contact with someone at the carrier's company or the telephone emergency call system (at present 999).

Whether or not these particular steps are called for, precautions are needed when delivering or collecting money by vehicle. These precautions include:

- From inside, observe the outside of the building when you are leaving to place cash in the vehicle. When in doubt about the presence of anyone or any vehicle, stay inside until egress is safe. If your doubts continue, call the police.
- Two people should be used to transport the cash – preferably both male, with one acting as observer as the other drives. Temporary or casual staff must not be used.
- Before setting off, contact the bank so that, once you arrive, they can make arrangements for the cash to be deposited without the need to join a queue.
- Before setting off, inform the local police of the transportation or collection of large amounts of cash and request their permission to park temporarily where restrictions apply.
- During the journey watch for any following vehicles. If suspicious, slow down and allow the vehicle to pass before making a detour

that will assist in confirming or alleviating suspicions. If suspicions are not alleviated, drive to the nearest police station and pass a description of the suspect vehicle, its registration number and descriptions of passengers to the police.

- Do not leave the vehicle at any time during the journey. If you come across an accident, if possible drive past. If stopped by the police, tell them that you will be happy to accompany them to the nearest police station, rather than compromise safety.

- When using busy streets and busy periods, vary routes and times as often as possible.

- Record the registration number of any vehicle that is noticed at the start or destination on consecutive journeys.

- Once at your destination, park as near to the bank as possible. Quickly transfer the cash into the bank with the observer keeping a look-out for anything or anyone suspicious. Once inside the bank the vehicle must be moved if there are parking restrictions directly outside the bank, unless prior arrangements have been made with the local police.

RECEPTION OF CASH FROM COMMERCIAL CARRIERS

It is becoming increasingly uncommon for wages to be paid in cash, but there are still companies and employees who prefer to pay and be paid that way. The majority of cash robberies nowadays take place inside buildings, particularly on the premises of the customer company, either at the time of cash delivery or immediately afterwards while the cash is still about. This is often done by gaining access to, and hiding on the premises. If it is possible to enter and hide, apart from the physical danger to security staff, it reflects very badly on their vigilance and efficiency. Certain precautions can be taken (other than the physical strengthening of the cash reception area) that any responsible company should consider adopting. These include:

- Immediately before the cash arrives, the entry route of the cash and any adjoining rooms should be checked for the presence of intruders.

- Outside doors and gates must be closed and locked behind the carriers.

- If on arrival there is the slightest cause for suspicion, the carriers should be warned to stay inside the safety of their vehicle and to inform their control of the situation.

- The carriers must not be given assistance to transport the cash into the cash reception area. It is their job, they are well trained, and confusion about responsibility could arise in the event of a loss. Other staff should keep a watching brief on what is happening and give assistance only when an incident occurs.

- At any time when strangers, on foot or in vehicles, are seen to take an undue interest in the proceedings, note particulars of those persons and any vehicles in use and pass these details on to the police.

- While waiting for the cash to arrive, admission to the immediate area of the cash reception should be restricted. No persons such as window cleaners, telephone engineers, contractors' staff and so on should be admitted until after the cash has been secured.

A robbery can happen on your premises and to staff personally. Familiarity with procedures is apt to lead cashier staff to disregard routine precautions. Security staff cannot afford to do this, and indeed they should try to impress on the people they are protecting the need for precautions.

COLLECTION OF CASH BY COMMERCIAL CARRIERS

This is most likely to be undertaken from retail premises where several of the precautions advocated above may not be practicable. While the ultimate responsibility rests with the carrier after signing for what has been taken away, such protective precautions as are feasible must, nevertheless, be implemented.

A respectable carrier must be used – that is, a carrier affiliated to one of the trade organisations such as the British Security Industry Association or the International Professional Security Association, or both. Impersonation of a bona fide carrier, using identical uniforms, is not unknown, but it is much more difficult for the robbers to acquire an identical vehicle, so parking away from a usual spot and out of sight is an immediate danger signal. Collection of cash is apt to become an accepted routine regarded with indifference. This should not be allowed to happen; unfamiliar carriers should be asked to produce proof that positively identifies them.

PENDING AND DURING PAYOUT OF WAGES

A security presence outside the room where wages are made up or checked is desirable to prevent the intrusion of unwanted visitors as well as potential robbers. A personal attack button located at the place where the security officer stands would be an advantage. The security officer must also:

- ensure that doors to the cash office are not casually left unlocked;
- check that money is not left lying about during meal breaks;
- be adequately briefed to recognise any breaches of normal procedures that might be suspect, because cash thefts can be perpetrated by staff who are tempted by a lax environment;
- remain sufficiently close to the payout point during pay packet issue in order to deter anyone contemplating a quick snatch or attempting to get another's pay packet by fraud or false signature.

OUT-OF-HOURS PRECAUTIONS

In most organisations, cash offices and safes are the obvious target for intruders as they offer the chance of immediately usable and rarely identifiable proceeds for their efforts. In this respect the security officer must:

- know exactly where all ready cash is held;
- know when cash is put into safes or strongrooms;
- know when cash is taken out for daily use;
- know the identity of all staff engaged in cash handling, especially those who have a normal right of entry into safes and strongrooms;
- make regular out-of-hours visits, carrying out physical checks to doors and locks during each visit;
- report any cash receptacle that is found open to the person responsible for its safekeeping, irrespective of the time of day.

ROBBERY: ACTIONS AND PROCEDURES

Action at the point of robbery

- do not resist the attacker and comply with their instructions;
- show your hands and avoid prolonged eye contact with the attacker;

- where possible, move away once you have complied with their instructions;
- if possible, note anything about the demeanour or characteristics of the attacker that might be useful to the police.

Post-robbery procedures

If a robbery has occurred, the following procedures must be adopted:

- notify the police;
- where there is injury, request an ambulance and apply first aid;
- protect the scene of the robbery;
- move persons who have been exposed to the robbery to a place of safety away from the scene, staying with them until the police arrive;
- obtain details of witnesses to the robbery;
- once the incident has been dealt with, consider post-robbery support for those involved, such as injury management or counselling.

6 Protection of Premises and Alarm Systems

PHYSICAL SECURITY MEASURES

Staff responsible for the security of premises must be familiar with the main types of equipment used for the protection of the premise and the site as a whole. The duties of the security officer are likely to include the checking of such precautions and ensuring that all the equipment is in good and efficient working order.

Perimeter walls

Walls are only protective as a result of their height. They should be built to a height of 2.4 m (8 feet) and the top should be surmounted by some other form of deterrent such as spikes or barbed or razor wire. Any disturbance of barbed wire will show whether there has been an intrusion, especially if the wire has been erected in close vertical loops. Barbed and razor wire must not be used below a height of 2.4 m (8 feet) and its use must be accompanied by signs indicating its presence. This may reduce liability should someone become injured because of its presence (see the 'Legal implications of security measures' section on page 72).

Fencing

Anti-intruder chain link fencing (BS 1722, Part 10, 1990)

The cheapest form of fencing is the wire mesh type, which may be plastic coated for durability. It is desirable that this type of fence complies with the minimum requirements as contained in BS1722, Part 10, 1990. Conventionally, it is fastened on to 1.8 or 2.4 m (6 or 8 feet) concrete posts topped by cranked arms carrying several strands of barbed wire. It is easily cut, bent down or pulled up for crawling under. It is difficult to maintain and is prone to becoming entangled in trees and shrubbery. In itself it offers little protection, but a good line of vision along the line of the fence coupled with good lighting and the use of CCTV might help to reduce the risk of intrusion.

It is important for the security officer to ensure when patrolling that all piled materials are kept away from the fence as these will provide a suitable climbing aid. Any fence that has become engulfed in trees and shrubbery or has been damaged must be reported and the details entered in the occurrence book.

Open mesh steel panel fencing (BS 1722, Part 14, 1990)

Welded mesh fencing is manufactured by welding the wire at its intersections. Expanded metal is produced from sheet metal that is slot-cut and stretched. The attack resistance of this type of fence is very much dependent on the gauge and mesh size of the wire. It is used in establishments with high security risks such as defence establishments and prisons, usually accompanied by coiled razor wire. Its specification should comply with the minimum requirements as contained in BS 1722, Part 14, 1990.

Security steel palisade fencing (BS 1722, Part 12, 1990)

This type of perimeter protection consists of pressed steel strips mounted 8 to 10 cm (3 to 4 inches) wide and is usually erected to a height of 3 m. It can be bolted on to a metal frame, which is then itself bolted to metal or concrete posts to form a very secure barrier. The top of each metal strip is forked as a deterrent against climbing and the bolt head can be burred to prevent unscrewing. This type of fence is suitable for being topped with anti-scaling devices such as revolving spikes. It should comply with the minimum requirements as contained in BS 1722, Part 12, 1990.

Gates

The number of entrances afforded to a site must be reduced to a minimum. Such entry points must be checked regularly during security patrols. Entrances that are not used must be sealed off to prevent unauthorised entry. General manufacturing requirements for gates should include the following:

- They must be no easier to climb than the adjoining fencing (and this should apply to the inside as well as the outside of the gate) and the top should be protected with wire or spikes.

- They must swing shut close to the ground to prevent someone crawling under.

- The means of suspension must be such so as to make it impossible for them to be lifted off bodily.

- Padlocks and shackles must be of good quality and the latter welded or bolted on to the gates with the bolts burred over.

- The gate area should be well lit.

- There must be an adequate aperture in a solid gate to enable a patrolling officer to see through.

Doors

Existing doors can be strengthened by adding steel sheeting (minimum 14 gauge) or substantial battens. Replacement doors should ideally be steel faced or manufactured from solid wood. The door jamb and surround must be as strong as the door itself and the door must be secured with a mortise deadlock of not less than five levers. Any padlock used must be of the close-shackle variety and its accompanying hasp should be of substantial manufacture.

Scotch tie or Gross Garnet hinges should be bolted through the door, not screwed into it, and the bolt ends should be hammered over. Glass panels in external doors should be kept to a minimum, and where used should be laminated, wired or protected by a shatter-resistant film.

Ram raids

Attacks by so called 'ram raiders' are a constant threat, particularly for retailers whose premises have high-value contents. Defences against this type of action include:

- the fitting of externally mounted roller shutters;

- the fitting of internally mounted roller shutters;

- the erection of concrete or steel bollards on pavements directly outside.

The erection of externally mounted features such as grilles, shutters and bars may require planning permission from the local authority. The local planning department must be consulted before they are installed. The erection of bollards on pavements may also be subject to approval by the local authority or the Highways Agency, who must be consulted before bollards are erected.

Internal doors

Solid doors and expensive locks are unnecessary unless the area or room contains something of real value. Once inside, a thief has ample time to smash down obstructions, and the damage that results may exceed the potential loss if the door had been left unlocked. However, insurance obligations may mean that all internal doors must remain locked when the premises are closed.

Double doors

The standing door should be kept bolted at the top and bottom by bolts recessed into the edge of the door.

Roller shutter doors

If roller shutter doors are to be fitted externally, they may require planning permission from the local authority or council. The doors can be operated manually by chain or electrically. The practice of securing such a door with a ring cemented into the floor and a padlock must not be used on electrically operated doors.

Concertina doors (Bolton type)

These are usually secured by a claw lock. This type of door can be strengthened by welding on lugs that can be secured by padlock to the door jamb. Where H girders are used as jambs, all the bolt heads holding the edge of the door must be burred over.

Fire exit doors

Security measures depend on what the fire authority is prepared to allow in the way of extra security locking at times when the premises are unoccupied. A choice of quick-release locking devices are available, some operated mechanically, others operated electrically with a built-in alarm when activated from the inside.

When patrolling, the security officer should ensure that all fire exit doors are properly shut and that the bolts locate properly in the door jamb or threshold.

Before installing new fire exit quick release mechanisms the advice of the local fire service should be sought.

Windows

If bars are to be recommended they should be spaced not more than 12.5 cm (5 inches) apart and a steel rod of minimum diameter 1.6 cm (5/8 inch) used. Cross-members must be fitted if the length of the window is such that bars could be sprung apart. Bars can be used on roof lights and fanlights, and can be in cradle shape if the window has to open for ventilation. Bars must be grouted into the surround of the window.

Prefabricated wire mesh can be a good substitute for bars, and shutters and grilles may also be fitted. Wired glass offers some protection where other means are not acceptable for amenity purposes, and it also has fire-containing value. Unused windows can be screwed up so they cannot be opened, and there are locks available for securing all types of openings.

Collapsible grilles are particularly suitable for shop premises and can be unobtrusive during opening hours. Toughened and laminated glass may be preferred in some applications, and some polycarbonate glazing substitutes can provide excellent resistance to breaking. Also, security films are available, designed to delay intrusion by holding the glass together.

Where roller shutters or grilles are used to protect glazing, local planning permission may be required if they are to be mounted externally.

Drain-pipes

Plastic pipes are cheaper to buy than metal. They do not need painting and the fittings are so light that they come off the wall when an attempt is made to climb them. Precautions that can be taken with metal pipes include:

- wrapping with barbed wire at a height of 2.4 m (8 feet) and above;
- fitting a half ring of downward-pointing spikes at 2.4 m;
- applying non-drying anti-climb paint (2.4 m and above).

Locks

Cylinder rim nightlatch (pin-tumbler lock)

Commonly known as the Yale lock, this type of lock has little security value other than the ability to restrict access by keeping internal doors secure. It has many key variations, is easily forced and is not accepted as a credible security device by insurance companies.

Box locks

Sometimes called rim locks, this type of lock fastens on to the surface of the door and its housing on the door jamb. Some special rim locks can be found in cell doors in police stations and in prisons, but in the main they are of a low security value and are more suited to the securing of domestic garages, sheds and storerooms.

Mortise locks

Mortise locks are set into the woodwork of the door and its jamb respectively. Provided that the structure of the door is solid, this type of lock provides considerable resistance to bodily forcing. Long metal striking plates recessed into the door jamb are an essential aid to the resistance capability of the lock. Generally, the more levers contained within the lock, the more key differs there are. For instance, a five-lever mortise lock will have in excess of 1000 key differs. When considering fitting a mortise lock, five levers are quoted as the minimum for insurance purposes. Some mortise locks are of the cylinder mortise type, and these can have many thousands of key differs.

Whatever type of mortise lock is fitted, it must comply with the requirements of BS 3621 (thief-resistant locks), 1980. Some locks of foreign origin are manufactured to a higher degree than those of the British kite-marked type.

Combination locks

These are frequently fitted to safe and strongroom doors. The dials have to be set to a predetermined combination of numbers before the lock will operate. A key lock can be incorporated in case the combination number becomes known by an unauthorised person.

Coded locks

These can be mechanically and electrically operated. This type of lock is accessed by punching in a series of number combinations into a key pad. This enables the bolt to be withdrawn manually by turning a knob, or electrically after selecting the correct code.

Some locks are operated by swiping a card through a card reader, which reads magnetically coded information from the card. The information is passed from the card to the reader and this will compare the received information with pre-programmed data and, if it matches, will allow access. These are often referred to as access control systems and can be used to monitor or restrict the movement of staff in certain areas.

Time locks

These are clock-operated to function only at a set time, and are usually used for safes and strongrooms. In addition, they normally incorporate an ordinary locking mechanism.

Padlocks

A very wide range of padlocks is available. For security purposes only those of the close-shackle variety should be used, and they must not have a locking mechanism of less than five levers. The shackle must not allow for a bar or lever to be inserted in order to force it. The hasps, staples and locking bars must be substantial and securely fixed if the effectiveness of the lock is not to be compromised.

Key-suited locks

Key-suited locks are made to a pre-planned system whereby a single master key opens all locks, sub-master keys open a specific number and ordinary keys open just one lock. So, for example, an executive holds a key that opens all doors in his or her jurisdiction, departmental heads can only open doors for their own sections and individuals can only open their own offices.

Key tabs

Note that if a sequence of keys and locks is changed, coloured and numbered key tabs are commercially available so that different colours can be allocated to separate departments and keys issued only to those presenting an appropriately coloured disk – this speeds up key issue and prevents mistakes.

Mirrors

Strategically placed mirrors can give improved visibility. They are extensively used inside retail stores to aid shop assistants and the like, but they should not be neglected for outside work.

CLOSED-CIRCUIT TELEVISION

CCTV cameras may be used in an infinite number of premises and locations as part of a simple or highly complex system that can be remotely controlled from a central point, usually a security office or company control room. CCTV cameras can reduce the amount of patrolling required and the officer is not immediately exposed to any of the dangers appearing on the CCTV monitor.

An officer must be fully trained with the CCTV equipment before becoming solely responsible for its use, and must appreciate exactly what action should be taken if an incident requiring a response takes place (including the video recording of such an incident).

The security officer must be conversant with the buildings and areas viewed by the CCTV system and the risks that might develop. A fixed camera with a single monitor, optionally coupled to a video recorder, may be used for individual risk targets, which might include:

- bank and building society counters
- bank vaults
- shop interiors and tills
- works entrances and reception areas
- computer rooms
- warehouse loading bays.

Cameras with remotely controlled pan and tilt facilities are useful in the following applications:

- viewing car parking areas
- viewing perimeter fences
- viewing the exterior of large buildings
- viewing general outside spaces.

For a wide and detailed view of an area, variable focusing enables 'zooming in' on any specific point. A stout outer housing will protect the cameras from the weather and vandalism, and a wash-and-wipe system on the front of the housing will keep the lens front clean. An automatic adjustment for variable light conditions can be incorporated into the lens and this may also protect the lens from the intense light of vehicle headlamps.

Low light or night viewing can be made possible by using an infra-red sensitive lens or by supplementing the cameras with infra-red lamps that enhance picture quality in low light conditions. Movement detectors can also be used to alert the control room that someone has entered the view of a fixed-position camera, but these are best used outside working hours when the site is not occupied by its workforce.

The whole set of cameras can be linked to the control panel by any number of cabling methods, enabling the operator to use a joystick to control the pan and tilt on the camera selected and to use push buttons to operate the wash-wipe system, zoom lens and other functions. Sequential switching allows the view from a number of cameras to be shown in turn on a single monitor, with a manual override available to stop the sequence and focus in on one location should the need arise. Conversely, systems are available that will allow any number of cameras (usually up to 16) to be viewed on one screen, with a facility that allows the operator to view any single screen selected.

A range of video recorders can be connected to the system to provide a permanent record, some activated by movement detector and some used with other alarm detector equipment. Other recorders allow for recording 24 hours a day, 7 days a week.

Each extra facility added to the basic installation adds to the cost, and every care must be taken to prevent the equipment being damaged by vandalism, or, in the control room, by carelessness or ignorance. Continual watching of the screen can be tiring for the officer, with a loss of concentration ensuing. Officers should have adequate rest periods between viewing and a relief officer should be available during break times.

INTRUDER ALARM SYSTEMS

The principle behind alarm systems is based on establishing a complete electrical circuit in the premises so that interference with any part causes an immediate alarm. Unless there are special provisions in the system, this alarm condition will continue to exist even if there is no further interference with any other part of the circuit. The result will be the sounding of alarm bells or the transmission of a signal indicating that the premises alarm has been activated.

Methods of giving alarm

An alarm may be given by the following means:

- A direct or shared line from a satellite to the alarm company central station. This is a very expensive means of alarm signalling and is only usually adopted at very high-risk security establishments. The direct line is continually monitored for line cuts or faults.

- An automatic sounding alarm bell that is fixed to an outer wall of the premises. These 'audible only' systems do not signal an outgoing message to the alarm company. They are designed to alert neighbouring premises only.

- A digital communicator or dialler, which dials a signal to the alarm company's central monitoring station. It is usually installed on an ex-directory outgoing-only telephone line so that the phone cannot be engaged and entry to the premises made without a signal being transmitted. If this line is cut the alarm will not signal.

- A protected telephone line. This line has the ability to transfer an alarm signal to another line if the original alarm line is interfered with. A further advantage is that it has cheaper annual costs than a direct line and can be installed on existing telephone lines. Also, the line can be used for other calls without compromising its ability to accept the alarm signal.

- Via an 'autodialler'. This equipment will automatically dial a number of keyholders in sequence when the alarm is activated. Police telephone numbers must not be entered into the autodialler because this form of transmitting an alarm signal is not acceptable to the police.

Police response

The police, subject to certain conditions, will respond to alarm calls received from the alarm company's central monitoring station. However, the Association of Chief Police Officers (ACPO) has introduced a policy governing when, where and which calls will be received and answered by the police. The policy has been brought in because of an unacceptable level of false calls received.

The ACPO policy is quite complex and is mainly a reference document for alarm installers and central monitoring stations. However, the document does contain implications for the end-user of an alarm system, for whom the policy can be broken down into three sections:

- levels of response
- withdrawal of response
- keyholders.

Levels of response

Type A

Type A is a remote signalling alarm system that is terminated at a recognised alarm-receiving station, remote video response centre or system operating centre for vehicles. All new alarm systems connected by remote signalling equipment to an alarm company central monitoring station will receive an immediate response until there have been three false alarm calls in any rolling 12-month period (subject to the nature, demand and priorities of the police).

Type B

With a type B system, the intruder alarm activation will require confirmation from a person at the scene that a criminal offence is in progress, which indicates that a police response is required. This will require human intervention, such as a member of the public, owner or agent visiting or viewing the premises. The addition of electrical means to provide confirmation will not promote such systems to type A. Police response to type B alarms is not guaranteed, and the level of response will be determined by the quality of information received.

Withdrawal of response

Following two false calls in any rolling 12-month period, the customer will be advised by the police in writing that urgent remedial action will need to be taken to avoid police response being withdrawn. Following three false calls in any rolling 12-month period, police response will be withdrawn, and the customer will be advised in writing of the requirement to stop the alarm company monitoring station forwarding alarm responses to the police. Response will not be reinstated automatically by the police: the conditions that will apply for reinstatement are not listed here but are available on the ACPO website. It is the subscriber's responsibility to apply to the police for reinstatement.

A false call is one that *has not* resulted from:

- a criminal attack or damage to the protected premises or an attempt at such;
- action by the emergency services in the execution of their duty;
- a call emanating from a personal attack button, initiated with good intent.

Keyholders

The police and the alarm installation company must be informed of changes to keyholders within 48 hours of taking over an existing system, of having a new system installed or when changing keyholders. Keyholders must:

- be telephone subscribers
- have transport
- be able to attend within 20 minutes of being notified.

The alarm monitoring station is responsible for maintaining a list of at least two keyholders and for their call-out after alarm activation. It is therefore very important that changes to keyholders are notified to them immediately.

ALARM COMPONENTS AND METHODS OF DETECTION

Control panel

Alarm system control panels have become more sophisticated as technology has advanced. The use of microchips has meant that many alarm control processes can now be carried out directly from the alarm monitoring station, including reset.

Personal attack buttons

All types of alarm can have personal attack buttons that will activate the alarm procedure despite the fact that the system as a whole is switched off. An example would be an attack on a bank or post office during normal working hours when a counter clerk could use the button without the knowledge of the attacker.

Methods of alarm detection

Door contacts

These are magnetic reeds which are fitted into the door and surround which are not visible without close scrutiny. When the alarm is set and the door opened the alarm activates.

Closed-circuit wiring

There are two types: (a) simple taut wiring protecting the backs of thin or hollow-core doors, vulnerable ceilings or walls; and (b) wiring contained in tubes mounted on a frame to protect windows. In each, fine non-stretch wire is used which breaks when moved.

Window foil

This is thin foil, which is stuck in a pattern around a window forming part of the alarm circuit. A break in the circuit caused by breaking glass will activate the alarm. Advancing technology has meant that this type of detection equipment is now rarely used.

Infra-red beams

This equipment sends an infra-red beam between a transmitter and a receiver. Anything interrupting the beam will break the circuit and activate an alarm. These are often fitted in high-security installations and can be used to activate outside lighting and to switch on CCTV cameras.

Vibration devices

These break a circuit when they react to vibration or shock waves. They are commonly found on windows where they detect jemmying, but they are also used on safes and strongrooms in the form of limpets.

Passive infra-red detectors

This is the most common type of intruder detector used in the alarm industry. It works on the principle of detecting body heat of warm-blooded animals. It is suitable to most applications, both commercial and domestic.

Ultrasonic detectors

These detectors involve the transmission of sound waves outside the range of human hearing. The apparatus is adjusted to its static surroundings and the introduction of any foreign body into the area causes the pitch to vary slightly, thereby creating an alarm condition. The system is mainly used in warehousing areas where other types of detectors may be obscured by stacked goods or shelving.

Break-glass detectors

These respond to the sound of breaking glass and can be calibrated to react only to the sound of breaking glass, making them unresponsive to outside influences such as high-pitched air brakes on goods vehicles.

Microwave detectors

These detectors operate on a similar principle to ultrasonic detectors, but they are not affected by air movement. This equipment is very rarely used in commercial applications, other than as part of a dual-technology detector.

Dual-technology detectors

These detectors are a combination of a passive infra-red detector and a microwave detector. They only generate an alarm when there is both movement and body heat, and are usually installed in draughty environments where a passive infra-red or microwave detector alone would generate false calls.

Audio detectors

This type of detector transmits sound back to the alarm company's central monitoring station. The system comprises a number of microphones strategically placed, which generate an alarm condition in response to noise, such as breaking glass, people walking about or voices. This equipment is very effective at determining whether an alarm call is genuine or not.

TVX-type cameras

These cameras are mounted adjacent to a traditional alarm detector. Once the detector has been activated the camera switches on, transmitting images back to the central monitoring station. The equipment is very effective in determining whether an alarm call is genuine or not.

Smoke-emitting devices

Smoke-emitting devices work alongside traditional types of detector. Once the detector is activated the room is filled with non-toxic smoke designed to disorientate an intruder.

Dye spray solutions

These substances are concealed in a canister and work alongside a traditional detector. On activation a fine spray is dispensed over the protected area and the intruder. The spray is identifiable (under laboratory test) to each premises in which it is installed. It will show up under ultra-violet light and will remain on suspects and their clothing for a considerable time.

Guard wire

Guard wire is a fibre-optic cable interwoven in fencing, which detects climbing, cutting or tampering with the fence. The wire can be used to induce an alarm condition or to switch on lighting or CCTV cameras.

LEGAL IMPLICATIONS OF SECURITY MEASURES

Occupiers' Liability Act 1984

This legislation has important implications for those charged with implementing new security measures. The Act (Section 2) states that an occupier of premises owes a duty of care to other people who may be in danger on those premises *whether they are there lawfully or not*. The Act says that if a person entering any premises (including where they are trespassing) is injured by any manufacturing process or equipment or as a result of any measure taken for the security of the premises, the occupier may be liable to prosecution if they are aware that the danger to other persons exists and that any person who is likely to enter into the vicinity of the danger could possibly be injured as a result (Section 3).

The Act further states (Section 5) that any duty of care owed may be discharged by taking reasonable steps to give warning of the danger concerned or to discourage persons from taking risks that might cause injury. This might include the display of warning signs, but occupiers' liability is not automatically avoided by putting up warning notices. However, a warning notice may, depending on the circumstances, sometimes be sufficient to discharge the duty.

In the absence of any judicial decisions on this Act, the implication of Section 3 is that any of the devices mentioned below would make the occupier liable if an intruder was injured due to their presence, even though such devices were within the perimeter of the premises. The following might be classed as involving such risks:

- anti-scaling devices
- barbed tape or razor wire
- anti-climb paint
- smoke-emitting intruder detectors.

Highways Act 1980, section 164

This section directs that where on land adjoining a highway there is a fence made with barbed wire on it, and the wire is a nuisance to persons using that highway, a notice may be served on the occupier of that land requiring him to abate the nuisance within a specified time, being not less than one month or more than six months from the date of serving of the notice.

For the purposes of this section, barbed wire means wire with spikes or jagged projections and it must be assumed that this includes barbed tape and razor wire.

These are deemed a nuisance to a highway if it is likely that a person or animal, lawfully using that highway will be injured by their presence. The general rule is that where this type of wire is being used, reasonable steps should be taken to prevent it causing injury. What is reasonable will depend on the facts of each case, but sensible siting will ensure that problems are not encountered. Barbed wire and tape should never be located at a height where people can easily come into contact with it without climbing.

7

Security and Vehicles

TRAFFIC MANAGEMENT

Creating efficient and speedy traffic movement and reducing acrimony over parking spaces for fellow employees is potentially one of the best public relations exercises that security officers can undertake. Motorists are sensitive about their driving and their manoeuvring ability, and about the parking privileges afforded to them by the company. Complaints about parking and vehicle matters should be taken seriously, no matter how trivial they appear at first sight. Responding to complaints may result in an improvement to the existing traffic movement system. If nothing can be done about the matter, or if the complaint is based on a wrong premise, the complainant should be so informed.

Vehicular accidents on company premises

Where private vehicles are involved in accidents on company premises, the matter is usually settled between the drivers themselves and their insurance companies. It can never be forecast, however, when some flaw in insurance cover or other peculiar circumstance may lead to the company being sued for negligence. It is necessary, therefore, for a brief note to be made for the company's records in case they are subsequently needed. The report should contain the following information:

- name, address, works number or company details of each driver;
- the time, date and precise location of the accident;
- the registration numbers and makes of the vehicles involved;
- details of the drivers' insurance companies if available (there is no legal obligation for them to be produced to security);
- the names and addresses of any witnesses;

- a brief description of the nature of the accident and any damage caused to the vehicles or other property;
- details of any injuries sustained to the drivers, passengers or any other people or animals.

If a company vehicle or property is involved, or there is any question of negligence by the company, these particulars should be amplified by including the following:

- any version of the accident that may have been proffered by either driver;
- similar versions that may have been given by witnesses;
- full details of insurance cover (where possible);
- a sketch-plan of the scene of the accident, showing the point of impact, the approach lines of the vehicles and any measurements taken;
- the state of the weather, road surface conditions and visibility;
- in the case of injury, the action taken on site to treat injuries and details of the disposal of the casualty.

In particular, anything that has been mentioned that has a bearing on possible negligence should be reported. Where company employees are witnesses or drivers and the matter is one of consequence, it is preferable to take their statements in writing if they agree to this.

Car park patrols

Occasional patrols of car parks should be carried out to:

- locate badly parked cars before their presence causes an obstruction;
- prevent theft from vehicles;
- provide a service to employees by notifying them of any lights left on, flat tyres and so on;
- notify of petrol or diesel oil leakage as a safety measure;
- note suspicious or possibly abandoned vehicles that may be of interest to the police and security services during times of heightened terrorist threat.

To give this service and to locate owners for any purpose, some form of register or computer database should be kept of vehicles that are regularly parked on the site. The database should contain the minimum information for its purpose, such as vehicle make, details of the owner or user, their works department, and telephone and extension number. Employees should be encouraged to report changes so that records can be kept up to date.

After dark, a company's private car park holds considerable attraction for a prospective theft of or from a motor car. The thief can reasonably assume that the owners will be engaged on shift work, or may know from observation what will be the earliest time the owners will go to their vehicles, thus giving ample time to carry out their crime.

For this purpose the intruder will have to move and make some noise, which may establish their presence. It follows that a security officer in many instances will achieve more by standing quietly, looking and listening, than by marching noisily up and down the rows of cars. Successful pursuit may be difficult, and one option is to pretend not to have noticed anything and return with assistance. Also, power of arrest available to people other than the police should be noted.

TRANSPORT PRECAUTIONS

Vehicles can be protected and common-sense precautions urged on drivers to prevent what can be the quickest, and perhaps most serious, type of theft that can be inflicted on a company.

Advice for drivers

Honest drivers are more interested than anyone in preserving their loads and will appreciate discussion and expert advice. Points that might be suggested to them include:

- Do not park up in quiet country lay-bys.

- Do not visit transport cafés where there are recurrent incidents or thefts.

- Use well-lit car parks for overnight parking. Do not leave vehicles in back streets near to lodgings for personal convenience.

- When in doubt, notify the police of the presence of your load. Do so in any case where a high-value load is involved.

- Check immobilisers, alarms and all door locks before leaving the vehicle for the night and sheet down loads tightly.

- If obliged to stop at an accident or by signals from the police, stay in the cab with the door bolted if in any doubts as to the bona fide nature of the situation. If you are unsure about the genuineness of the police officer, indicate that you will be happy to follow on to the local police station.

- If your own vehicle is engaged in an accident, use your discretion as to whether you should get out. If in doubt, stay inside and insist that the police are called.

- Do not carry casual passengers or hitch-hikers. There may be an insurance problem if they get injured.

- View with suspicion any waving and flashing of lights to indicate faults with your vehicle, and ignore any diversionary messages left at cafés.

- Report to the police and your employer any approaches from strangers attempting to steal the load with your connivance.

WEIGHBRIDGE FRAUDS

Collusion between a weighbridge operator and a driver to defraud can continue for a considerable time before any suspicion arises. It will usually take the form of the operator falsifying the figures he or she records. The weighbridge operator may deliberately allow a malpractice by the driver to inflate the tare weight when collecting materials, or the gross weight when delivering. It has been known for an operator–supplier or operator–customer liaison to exist profitably without the knowledge of the driver where the operator could produce false tickets.

Weighing is a brief, impersonal operation, and if a driver spends too much time being convivial in the weigh-office, the fact should be duly noted and quiet observations kept. An out-of-hours check of the records might well show, for instance, that a vehicle's tare differs when another driver brings it in.

Fraud can be carried out without the knowledge of the weighman by the empty vehicle registering a higher empty weight than it should. There are a number of ways to achieve this. They include:

- fitting a large spare petrol tank or carrying drums filled with water that are emptied after weighing;

- where the lorry has sideboards and tailboards, having a 'bowed' tarpaulin carrying water that is tipped off before loading; and similarly, where a welded body, tipper-type lorry is used, having water in the bottom that is tipped before loading;

- carrying paving stones, old spare wheels, skids, tarpaulins and so on to be discarded;

- remaining in the cab during weighing, or having pets or family in the cab;

- drivers standing outside the office window but having their feet on the weighbridge;

- where the same vehicle delivers repeatedly to a site and only weighs empty at the beginning of each day, dropping a spare wheel after the first delivery and picking it up at the end of the day.

It will be obvious that the sight of a visiting driver surreptitiously disposing of anything of negligible value but considerable weight from his vehicle should arouse suspicion. The tricks used to inflate a tare can of course be used to inflate a gross when delivering, and in some trades the load itself may be soaked with water to give it an apparent higher weight. A false, reduced tare can also be induced by marginally overlapping the edge of the bridge with the wheels.

The profits that can accrue are such that well-planned frauds may be considered worthwhile. For example, where a tare weighing is only carried out at the beginning of the day in which a number of collections are made with the same vehicle, a similar but lighter vehicle with identical plates can be substituted. Where skips are in use, skips of identical appearance with the same figures on them but of different weights can be substituted as required so as to obtain an advantageous weight for the supplier or customer.

There are advantages in having the security department responsible for weighbridge operations. The company's profitability may be closely related to this policy.

If fraud is suspected a check of the weighbridge books, as mentioned earlier, should show whether a vehicle's empty weight remains constant. Observations should be kept on suspect drivers and, if the trick is seen, the driver should be allowed to load and go over the weighbridge to be weighed out. If the driver then accepts the weights, the offence is complete and the driver will have no defence if something deliberate has been seen to be done to increase the empty reading.

If collusion between the driver and the weighman is suspected, consider police assistance rather than a spot check. A mistake in weighing could prove a good defence and it would be better to try and find out what is done with the excess material.

VEHICLE SEARCH

If the searching of vehicles is authorised or is to be conducted with the consent of the user, or if theft is strongly suspected, make the search thorough and methodical, bearing in mind places where property may be hidden, some of which are listed in the following sub-sections (and not forgetting the driver's person if small but valuable items are concerned). A few such searches are a better deterrent than more searches of a casual nature.

Private cars

Places where property might be hidden include:

- beneath the removable back seat;
- underneath the front seats;
- in the webbing under the front seats;
- under paper or other materials in glove compartments and door pockets;
- under carpets;
- in the tool box or under the boot floor covering;
- under, behind or in the spare wheel, particularly if it is carried underneath the boot;
- where the boot has hardboard or similar side panelling, between the panelling and the outer skin of the car; the screws or clips holding the panelling in place may show that the piece has been removed, and rocking the car may show whether anything heavy is hidden;
- wedged behind the battery under the bonnet;
- tied to a chassis member or the exhaust underneath.

In a close search, always look underneath the vehicle. It is not unknown for a special compartment to have been made under the floor. Also, where small and valuable items are concerned, do not forget the less likely places such as inside the heater tubes and in the wiring under the dashboard. The extent of the search must depend on what is at risk and the degree of suspicion.

Commercial vehicles

Hiding places include:

*   under seats (a favourite place to put half-paving stones before going over the weighbridge empty);
*   inside the spare wheel;
*   under tarpaulins or skids on the platform of the lorry;
*   on top of the cab or inside;
*   wedged under or along chassis members;
*   inside lengths of scaffolding;
*   where a vehicle is nearly fully loaded, tight against the tailboard where the material is difficult to see.

When using a ladder to look inside or on top of a high-sided lorry, ask the driver to stop the engine and get out of the cab to watch what you are doing. 'Accidents' have been known to happen where a lorry has moved. Where a mechanical shovel has been used to work inside premises, it is conventional for it to leave with the shovel raised to a safe position. Occasionally the driver must be made to lower the shovel for inspection because this is a useful place to carry stolen property.

MISCELLANEOUS FRAUDS INVOLVING TRANSPORT

*   Drivers of fictitious transport companies calling to solicit a cheap return load to main centres. If the transport manager is silly enough to accept this sort of offer, check the documents and vehicle as thoroughly as possible before it leaves.

*   Collusion between the driver and warehouse staff to place extra material on a vehicle carrying customers' orders. Action should be carefully considered to prevent the offender offering the explanation of having made a genuine mistake. It is better to arrange for the vehicle to be followed. This may continue for some time before a deficiency is noticed. Familiarity between driver and warehouseman, and evidence of their possessing an unusual amount of money, may give an indication.

*   Drivers putting extra on their vehicles before leaving. The driver who always comes into work early is the one to watch.

- The unknown caller with a vehicle and an 'appointment' with some person in the works that necessitates bringing the vehicle in. Check that the person named is available and knows the caller.

- Warehouse staff taking advantage of poor systems to produce unofficial documentation to authorise loading of materials, then destroying copies so that no record of the transaction remains. Alternatively, when compiling documents, taking out carbons and subsequently making amendments on duplicates so that an excess may be loaded but not charged to the conspiring customer. Irregularities in alignment, spacing and writing on notes may give rise to suspicion of this. Any good sequential system of documentation should stop the chance of these happening.

- Warehouse staff signing for loads or goods that have never been received.

- Property of value removed in rubbish skips and swill containers from canteens under cover of contents.

- Property taken out alongside equipment of regular contractors on the premises – for example, among window cleaners' ladders and buckets.

8 Law of Theft and Related Offences

The law relating to stealing is contained in the Theft Act 1968. This Act has proved to be one of the least ambiguous pieces of criminal legislation ever produced. A knowledge of its basic content is essential for the professional security officer.

Only certain sections and parts of the Act that are likely to be concerned in the performance of security duties are outlined, and the text extracts from the Act are summaries rather than verbatim quotations.

THEFT ACT 1968

Section 1: basic definition of theft

A person is guilty of theft if he dishonestly appropriates property belonging to another with the intention of permanently depriving the other of it.

It is immaterial whether the appropriation is made with a view to gain or is made for the thief's own benefit, and it must be intended to deprive the owner of the property permanently.

It follows that there are four salient points that must be proved if an offence is to be successfully prosecuted. These are explained in the subsequent sections of the Act. The four points are:

- dishonesty on the part of the accused (Section 2);
- an appropriation (taking) of the property by the accused (Section 3);
- the property belongs to a person other than the accused or his or her spouse (Section 5);
- the intention of the accused to permanently deprive the owner of the property (Section 6).

Section 4 of the Act defines the term 'property'.

Section 2: dishonest

A person's appropriation of property belonging to another is not to be regarded as dishonest if the person: (a) appropriates the property in the belief that he has a right in law to deprive the other of it on behalf of himself or a third party; (b) appropriates the property in the belief that he would have had the consent of the other if the other knew of the circumstances of the appropriation; (c) appropriates the property in the belief that the person to whom the property belongs cannot be discovered by taking reasonable steps.

(a) and (b) are the old 'claim of right made in good faith' – one of the protestations to be expected from thieves wishing to evade the consequences of their actions. The facts may render the explanation absurd, but if the belief is genuine, even though mistaken, an apparent suspect may subsequently be acquitted. A security officer must therefore give the thief every chance to offer an explanation – what is said may be so transparently false that this in itself may ensure a conviction.

Element (c) refers to 'stealing by finding'. What constitutes reasonable steps may depend on the nature of what has been found and on the circumstances of the find. To keep possession of a wage packet bearing the owner's name or a labelled carton found by the roadside, and with it a failure to take even the simplest of steps to return the property to the true owner, clearly shows dishonesty. Technically, property found on premises should revert to the owners of the premises if the true owner cannot be traced, but the general and least controversial practice is to let the finder retain it in those circumstances.

Section 3: appropriation

Any assumption by a person of the rights of an owner amounts to an appropriation, including where a person has come by the property (innocently or not) without stealing it. Any later assumption of a right to it by keeping or dealing with it as an amounts to appropriation.

It is immaterial how, when and in what circumstances the appropriation is effected.

This section provides for theft by a person who has possession of property with the permission of the owner – for example as bailee; by one who finds property and knows or can find the owner; by one who acquires it by mistake of another (the goods delivered to a wrong address); and by parents of a child under the age of criminal responsibility who brings stolen goods home which they knowingly accept.

Section 4: property

Property includes money and all other property, real or personal, including things in action and other intangible property.

The forms of property that are deemed cannot be stolen are of a nature unlikely to be of interest in security practice, such as wild creatures, land, crops growing wild and so on.

Section 5: belonging to another

Property shall be regarded as belonging to any person having possession or control of it or having in it any proprietary right. It is not necessary that the person from whom the property is stolen is the actual owner.

Where a person receives property from or on account of another and is under an obligation to the other to retain and deal with that property in a particular way, the property or the proceeds shall be regarded as belonging to the other.

Where a person gets property by another's mistake and is under an obligation to make restoration, an intention not to make restoration shall be regarded as an intention to deprive that person of the property.

A partner can steal from a partnership and an owner can steal his own property – for example, where a car has been put into a garage for repair and the owner takes it away without paying for the repair or by breaking in to the garage or by subterfuge; or where material entrusted by a contractor to a subcontractor for work to be done on it and then returned, but is converted by the contractor to his own use.

Section 6: intention of permanently depriving

A person who appropriates property belonging to another without meaning the other to permanently to lose the thing itself is nevertheless to be regarded as having the intention of permanently depriving the other of it if the person's intention is to treat the thing as their own to dispose of regardless of the other's rights.

It is no defence to return property purely because responsibility for the theft has been established and the culprit hopes to avoid the consequences of doing so. The offence is also equally committed if the property is abandoned where the owner has no hope of finding it, or it is left in such a condition that it is of no further use to anyone.

A principle of general application worth bearing in mind is the doctrine of 'recent possession' – where newly stolen property is found in the possession of an individual, he can be convicted of the theft of it.

Section 7: punishment for theft

A person guilty of theft shall on conviction of indictment be liable to imprisonment for a term not exceeding ten years.

'On indictment' is when an accused is tried before a judge and jury at a Crown Court. The maximum sentence of imprisonment a magistrate can impose for one offence is six months.

Section 8: robbery

A person is guilty of robbery if he steals and, immediately before or at the time of doing so, uses force on any person or puts or seeks to put any person in fear of being then and there subjected to force.

The use of force or threat of it must be aimed at effecting the theft and must be used immediately before the theft or at the time of the theft, not after the theft has been carried out in order to escape. Where someone has been assaulted after the theft has taken place, the appropriate offences may well be theft and assault. Firing a gun to intimidate is use of force.

A person guilty of robbery or of an assault with intent to rob is liable to imprisonment for life.

Section 9: burglary

Section 9 (1)(a) states:

A person is guilty of burglary if he enters a building or part of a building as a trespasser with intent to: (a) steal from within that building or part of the building; (b) rape any woman in that building or part of a building; (c) inflict grievous bodily harm on any person in that building or part of the building; (d) cause damage to that building, part of the building or anything therein.

Section 9 (1)(b) states:

A person is guilty of burglary if having entered a building or part of a building as a trespasser he (a) steals or attempts to steal anything therein or (b) inflicts or attempts to inflict grievous bodily harm on any person therein.

If the person has with him at the time of committing burglary any firearm, imitation firearm, weapon of offence or explosive, that person is guilty of aggravated burglary (Section 10). 'Imitation firearm' means anything that has the appearance of a firearm, whether capable of being discharged or not.

Permitted entry by a fraudulent means comes within the scope of the section 9. For example, any entry gained on the pretext say, of being a gas inspector, where permission to enter premises is induced by deceit has entered those premises as a trespasser because true consent is not given.

The old concept of burglary is considerably expanded. The time of day that it is committed is immaterial, and all buildings are covered, including, for example, caravans or houseboats that are lived in permanently. People legitimately within a building can commit burglary by entering a section of it where they are not permitted to go – for example, a hotel guest stealing from another guest's bedroom. It will be noted that the intent must be to do or attempt to do one of four things:

- commit theft
- inflict grievous bodily harm
- rape any woman
- cause damage.

Section 11: removal of articles from places open to the public

It is an offence for any person to take without lawful authority or reasonable excuse the whole or part of any article displayed or kept for display to the public within a building or within its grounds to which the public have been given access to view.

The offence carries a maximum penalty of five years imprisonment on indictment. Proof of intent to permanently deprive the owner of the property is not necessary as the temporary unauthorised taking of an article from the building or its grounds is adequate to prove the offence. This section is of particular interest to security professionals who work in museums, stately homes and temporary art exhibitions. The offence can only be committed when the premises or grounds are open to the public. In other circumstances, other offences will apply. Collections assembled purely for sale are excluded.

Section 12: taking a motor vehicle or other conveyance without authority

A person shall be guilty of this offence if without having the consent of the owner or other lawful authority he takes away any conveyance for his own or another's use or knowing that any such conveyance has been so taken drives it or allows himself to be carried in or on it.

A conveyance means anything constructed for the carriage of a person or persons, whether by land, sea or air.

If the taker genuinely believes that the owner's consent would have been granted, had the owner known of the circumstances of the taking of the conveyance, no offence is committed.

Section 13: abstracting electricity

This section describes the offence of dishonestly using electricity or causing it to be wasted or diverted.

Section 15 and 16: obtaining property or a pecuniary advantage by deception

These offences have been repealed by the Fraud Act 2006 (see Chapter 9).

Section 17: false accounting

A person who dishonestly with a view to gain for himself or another destroys defaces, conceals or falsifies any account or record or any document made or required for any accounting purpose or produces or makes use of any such account which is or maybe misleading, false or deceptive commits the offence.

This offence is not limited in application to employees as against their employers. It is of general application, but only relates to documents used for accounting purposes. A clock card is such a document, so clocking offences could be charged under this section.

Section 21: blackmail

Any person who with a view to gain for himself or another makes any unwarranted demand by menaces commits an offence, unless: (a) the person who does so has reasonable grounds for making the demands and (b) that the use of menaces is a proper means of reinforcing the demand.

Menaces have been interpreted as including threats of injury to persons or property and of accusing a person of misconduct. The menaces can be in writing, speech or conduct.

Section 22: handling stolen goods

A person handles stolen goods if knowing or believing them to be stolen he dishonestly receives them or dishonestly undertakes to assist in their retention, removal, disposal or realization, by or for another's benefit.

A child under ten cannot legally steal and therefore there cannot be a handling charge against parents who accept the property, but a charge of theft may be brought against them.

Physical possession of the property is not necessary provided the person charged controlled its movement or disposal. Actual knowledge that property has been stolen no longer needs to be proven if the circumstances are such that the handler must have believed it was and deliberately ignored this fact.

Section 23: advertising rewards

A loser (and the person who publishes) can commit an offence by advertising a reward for the return of stolen goods with a promise of no questions asked or immunity from arrest or inquiry.

Section 25: going equipped for stealing

A person shall be guilty of this offence if, when not at his own place of abode he has with him any article for use in the course of or in connection with any burglary, theft or cheat.

If an article has been specially made for a criminal purpose, proof of possession will be adequate evidence of the purpose – for example, the possession of skeleton keys or balaclava helmets cut with mouth and eyeholes to form masks. The circumstances will have to indicate the intent where more common articles are used, such as gloves, torches, screwdrivers, chisels, baseball bats and so on.

Power of arrest

With the exception of the offences under Section 25 above and Section 12 (taking a motor vehicle or other conveyance without authority) all the offences under the Theft Act carry sentences that make them indictable offences, which means that they are offences for which any person may make an arrest, subject to the conditions stated in Chapter 10 under the heading 'Arrest by a person other than a constable'. However, under Section 12 the offence is only indictable if the vehicle-taking is aggravated – for example, if the vehicle is involved in a road accident, set on fire or damaged in some other way.

THEFT IN SCOTLAND

The Theft Act 1968 does not apply in Scotland, where stealing is a common law offence. Nevertheless, the necessary constituents are virtually identical, although different terminology is used. However, the age of criminal responsibility is 8 years, not 10 years as in England, meaning that there is a presumption that a child under 8 years cannot be guilty of an offence.

9 Other Relevant Criminal Law

FRAUD

The Fraud Act 2006 repeals a number of offences that are currently legislated for under the Theft Acts of 1968 and 1978, and creates new offences. The 1968 Theft Act offences repealed include:

- obtaining property by deception (Section 15)
- obtaining a money transfer by deception (Section 15A)
- obtaining a pecuniary advantage by deception (Section 16).

The Theft Act 1978 offences repealed include:

- obtaining services by deception (Section 1)
- evasion of liability (Section 2).

The new Act creates a number of offences, including:

- fraud
- fraud by false representation
- fraud by failing to disclose information
- fraud by abuse of position
- possession of articles for use in fraud
- participating in fraudulent business
- obtaining services dishonestly.

The Act seeks to address and change the way that fraud cases are dealt with to take account of changes in technology.

CRIMINAL DAMAGE

With certain exceptions concerning railways and shipping, the Criminal Damage Act 1971 consolidated all previous legislation connected with damage caused deliberately or by completely reckless behaviour. Its provisions do not extend to Scotland and Northern Ireland but the basics are identical, and in the former it is referred to as malicious mischief (a common law offence).

The Criminal Damage Act 1971 has three sections creating the offences of destroying and damaging property, destroying or damaging property with intent to endanger life, and threats to damage or destroy property and the possession of anything with intent to destroy or damage property.

Section 1(1): destroying or damaging property

A person who without lawful excuse destroys or damages any property belonging to another, intending to destroy or damage any such property or being reckless as to whether any such property would be damaged or destroyed shall be guilty of an offence.

Section 1(2): destroying or damaging property (aggravated)

A person who without lawful excuse destroys or damages any property whether belonging to himself or another, intending to destroy or damage any such property or being reckless as to whether any such property would be damaged or destroyed and (a) intending by the destruction or damage to endanger the life of another or (b) being reckless as to whether the life of another would be thereby endangered shall be guilty of an offence.

Section 1(3): damage by fire

An offence under this section by destroying or damaging property by fire shall be charged as arson (see below).

Lawful excuse

This can be defined as follows:

• At the time of committing the acts the person believed that consent had been given by the person responsible for the property or consent would have been given if the person responsible for the property had known of the actions and the consequences.

- That the person's actions were designed to protect property or the rights or interests of the property belonging to himself or another and at the time the person honestly believed that they were in immediate need of protection and the actions used or intended were reasonable having regard to all the circumstances.

These excuses are intended to cater for mistakes and incidents such as breaking down doors and demolition to stop the spread of fire.

'Arson' is the term used when someone wilfully and without lawful excuse sets fire or attempts to set fire to a building or anything or anyone in it or against it. To sustain a prosecution under the Act it must be shown that there was an intention, actual or constructive, to commit the offence. However, when a person knows that what he is doing will probably set fire to a building and is recklessly unconcerned as to whether it does or does not, he can be convicted.

Security officers should watch bystanders at a suspicious outbreak of fire and note any behaviour that seems out of keeping with the occasion, or the presence of someone who has been present at previous incidents. There is evidence that pyromaniacs like to remain at the scene in order to watch the results of their actions.

Power of arrest

All the offences under the Criminal Damage Act 1971 are punishable with at least ten years' imprisonment. It follows therefore that all are indictable offences and any person, including security officers, may carry out an arrest subject to the arrest conditions (see Chapter 10).

Compensation

After the conviction of an offender the convicting court may make a compensation order in addition to any other sentence it may pass. It is advisable in criminal damage cases for the claimant to have documented the full costs of making good the damage, so as to provide information requested by the court. Such information should include labour costs as well as the costs of materials. Some complainants in damage cases exaggerate their loss so it is as well to be equipped with the precise details as there are limits to the amounts that a court can award.

OFFENCES AGAINST THE PERSON

Under the Offences Against the Person Act 1861, an assault is constituted by any attempt to apply unlawful force to another. 'Battery' includes touching and laying hold, however trifling, of another's person or clothes in an angry, rude, insolent or hostile manner. If done by accident or with lawful consent it would not constitute an assault and battery.

Assaults are divided into the following categories depending on the severity of injury (and, unless stated otherwise, all section numbers refer to the Offences Against the Person Act 1861).

Section 39 Criminal Justice Act 1988: common assault

Common assault and battery shall be summary offences and a person guilty of them shall be liable to a fine or to imprisonment not exceeding six months, or to both.

This offence usually arises out of 'fisticuffs' resulting in minor bruising or bleeding. If the assault takes the form of resistance to a legal arrest it can become a more serious matter altogether.

Section 47: assault occasioning actual bodily harm

'Actual bodily harm' is any hurt or injury calculated to interfere with the health or comfort of the victim and it includes any nervous or hysterical condition resulting from an assault. Examples of bodily harm include bruising, minor wounds and sprains and strains. There is no need to prove an intention to occasion the actual bodily harm caused, or even whether the accused had foresight of it. Obviously it would be better to prove intent or foresight where possible.

This offence carries a maximum prison sentence of five years and is therefore an indictable offence.

Section 18: wounding with intent to do grievous bodily harm

Whosoever shall unlawfully and maliciously by any means whatsoever wound or cause grievous bodily harm to any other person with intent to do grievous bodily harm to any person or with intent to resist or prevent the lawful apprehension or detention of any person' commits an offence.

Wounding involves an actual breaking of the skin, with or without a weapon, by an assault that the assailant is bound to know will cause serious injury. Grievous bodily harm would include a very serious injury such as a skull fracture.

This offence carries life imprisonment and is therefore an indictable offence.

Section 20: inflicting bodily injury, with or without a weapon

Whoever shall unlawfully and maliciously wound or inflict grievous bodily harm upon any other person either with or without a weapon or instrument commits an offence.

This offence carries a maximum prison sentence of five years therefore it is an indictable offence.

In cases of substantial injury, ambulance assistance will be required and routine police attendance will follow. Security action to some extent will be dictated by the circumstances, such as the use of a weapon, the extent of injuries and the wishes of the complainant. Wounding and grievous bodily harm are indictable offences, and therefore there is a power of arrest, subject to the arrest conditions discussed in Chapter 10. Weapons should be retained with minimum handling. Persons should be excluded from the scene of a serious assault until police clearance is given, and every effort should be made to identify witnesses or those who have information. If the assault involves serious injury it will be important to protect the scene of the crime until the police arrive, possibly involving security staff cordoning off the area.

INDECENT ASSAULT

The offence against a woman falls under Section 14(1) of the Sexual Offences Act 1956 and against a man under Section 15(1). Allegations of such offences raise several difficulties for security officers. The course of action will depend on the wishes of the victim, but it is usually necessary for the police to become involved.

Indecent assault is 'an assault accompanied by circumstances of indecency'. There is no corresponding definition of indecency and its meaning has to be that which would be given it by a reasonable person – would the actions be regarded as intentionally indecent and offensive to the modesty and feelings of the victim?

The maximum sentence permitted under the Act is ten years' imprisonment, so it is indictable, carrying a power of arrest that is available to persons other than the police.

Legally, persons under 16 years of age and mental defectives cannot consent to an indecent assault upon themselves.

Should the security officer receive a complaint of indecent assault, or indeed any other sexual offence, the police should be called even if it is against the wishes of the victim. The security officer must note a number of crucial points that will assist the police when they arrive, including:

- the manner in which the complaint was made;
- any initial words or statement made by the complainant;
- the state, demeanour and appearance of the complainant;
- the time, date and place of the complaint;
- any sources of corroboration and details of witnesses.

It is important when receiving such a complaint that another person is present; that person being of the same sex as the complainant. Also, it may be desirable, if the complainant wishes to, inform a member of their immediate family, and this must be done if the victim is under 16 years of age.

It is also important that the human resources and welfare departments of the company are involved. The victim may require some counselling as a result of the incident and these departments are in the best position to give such help.

Allegations of sexual harassment or harassment generally that fall short of actual acts of indecency may pose more problems for the security officer – problems that might be better dealt with by the human resources or welfare departments.

HARASSMENT

All types of harassment, including those within the workplace, come under the Protection From Harassment Act 1997. This legislation was brought in to deal with situations where people are victims of obsessive harassment, sometimes referred to as stalking. Under this legislation, harassment also extends to receiving unwanted gifts or mail, and even abusive telephone calls, provided the 'harassment' occurs on more than one occasion.

The provisions of the Act make it possible for the police and victims to take action at an early stage. The offences under the Act may be committed anywhere and all are indictable, except for the Section 1 and 2 offence. Therefore, subject to the arrest conditions described in Chapter 10, a person other than the police may arrest. There is no requirement under the Act to prove specific intent to cause harassment.

Sections 1 and 2: causing harassment

A person must not pursue a course of conduct which amounts to the harassment of another and which the offender knows or ought to know amounts to the harassment of another.

The points to prove are that the suspect has pursued a course of conduct that has occurred on a least two occasions, that the conduct amounted to the harassment of another person and that the suspect knew or ought to have known that the conduct amounted to harassment. The person whose course of conduct is in question ought to know that it amounts to harassment if a reasonable person in possession of the same information would think the course of conduct amounted to harassment. On conviction, a person is liable to six months' imprisonment, a fine or both.

Section 3: the civil remedy

Section 3 of the Act states that a person who is in breach of Sections 1 and 2 may be the subject of a claim in civil proceedings by the person who is or who maybe the victim of the course of conduct in question. On such a claim, damages may be awarded for any anxiety caused by the harassment and any resulting financial loss. In such proceedings, the high or county court will issue an injunction restraining the assailant from continuing the harassment. A breach of the injunction is an indictable offence carrying a maximum of five years' imprisonment.

Section 4: putting people in fear of violence

A person whose course of conduct causes another to fear on at least two occasions that violence will be used against that person and which offender knows or ought to know that the course of conduct will cause another to fear violence on each of those two occasions is guilty of an offence.

This course of conduct which causes another to fear on at least two occasions that violence will be used against them represents the major difference between the Section 4 and the Section 1 and 2 offence. 'Violence' is not defined but it is clearly significantly more serious than 'harassment', and the violence feared may be violence directed towards the victim or against property.

Section 5: restraining orders

Section 5 of the Act is not of particular importance to the security officer. It deals with powers of the courts to place restraining orders on a person who has been convicted under the Act. The restraining order is designed to prevent further conduct that amounts to harassment or conduct that will cause a fear of violence, and will prohibit the offender from doing anything that is so described in the order. The order granted will be for a specific period or until a further order is granted.

Breach of a restraining order is a criminal offence punishable by a maximum of five years' imprisonment. Therefore, a power of arrest for persons other than the police is available (Chapter 10).

BRIBERY AND CORRUPTION

Bribery is the offering or receiving by any person of any undue reward in order to induce them to do, or to reward them for doing something contrary to the rules of honesty and integrity. The offer of a bribe constitutes an attempt to bribe. Most people believe that bribery concerns only an employee in a government or other public body, or the police, but the Prevention of Corruption Act 1906 extends to persons in all types of employment.

Section 1: accepting inducements and rewards

Any agent who corruptly accepts from any person any gift or consideration as an inducement or reward for doing or forbearing to do any act in relation to his principal's affairs or business or any person who corruptly gives, agrees to give or offers such a gift or consideration for so doing is guilty of an offence.

'Agent' includes any person employed by or acting for another. Security officers are especially open to corruption and should at once report to their superiors any approach that appears to be made with that intention, taking care not to show to the person making the approach that this is going to be done.

Corruption in commercial and industrial businesses is most commonly encountered in the awarding of contracts and the purchase of materials, but also in the illegal or unethical obtaining of business information or in forms where the end product is essentially theft. Should a security officer receive information alleging that this is happening, he or she must regard it as strictly confidential, to be divulged to and discussed only with his superiors. Obtaining adequate evidence may require long-term planning and observation.

FORGERY

The principal legislation regarding forgery is the Forgery and Counterfeiting Act 1981.

Section 1: making of a false instrument

A person is guilty of forgery if he makes a false instrument with the intention that he or another shall use it to induce somebody to accept it as genuine and by reason of so accepting it to do or not to do some act to his own or any other person's prejudice.

The offence carries ten years' imprisonment and is therefore an indictable offence.

Altering a genuine document, or making a false document in order that they appear genuine, is forgery. The definition extends beyond the mere forging of a signature. The actual use of a forged document is called 'uttering' and this is an offence additional to the forgery.

The forging of money orders, share certificates and passports is covered in Section 5 of the Act, and the schedule to that section extends it to cheque and credit cards, ordinary and travellers' cheques, which are of interest to those in retail security. Being in possession of special paper and printing facilities with intent to make such items is also an offence. 'Instrument' includes any document, formal or informal, GPO revenue stamps, discs, tapes or soundtracks on which information may be recorded or stored (Section 8).

Counterfeiting banknotes or coins intending to pass them as genuine, or knowingly having them or tendering them carries the same penalty as forgery – ten years maximum on indictment, conferring a power of arrest for persons other than the police. It should be noted that even the frivolous making of coins or notes without intent to use them as genuine is an offence carrying a penalty of up to two years' imprisonment.

The forms of forgery usually encountered by security officers involve the alteration of figures on documents and requisitions to obtain goods or materials, the forgery of a signature to obtain another person's wage packet, and alterations to accounts and to receipts produced for payments from petty cash. Major forms of forgery are likely to be referred to the police fraud squad at an early stage.

COMPUTER MISUSE

Provided there is good access control to computer suites, security officers are unlikely to become involved with them, but it has been known for aggrieved persons to do serious damage to machines. The offence is then the obvious one of criminal damage and, according to the circumstances of entry, burglary. However, so much publicity has been given to the security dangers associated with computers that brief comment is necessary.

Computers can be used for theft and fraud in the same way as other forms of recording can be exploited, but there used to be instances where the legislation proved inadequate to bring offences to justice. The Computer Misuse Act 1990 closed many loopholes by creating new offences. Section 1 concerns using a computer to knowingly secure unauthorised access to any program or data held in any computer. Section 2 aggravates that offence if the person has an accompanying intent to commit or facilitate the commission of an offence by himself or someone else even if the offence proves impossible. Section 3 covers the person who, with requisite knowledge and intent, makes unauthorised changes to the content of any computer or disrupts its usage; planting a virus in a computer program would come under this category.

A security officer should note any unusual out-of-hours presence in the computer suite by a computer staff member: they should be challenged and their reason for being there should be verified.

TRESPASS

Trespass is examined under three headings: civil, criminal and aggravated trespass.

Civil trespass

Trespass is not normally a criminal offence, but it constitutes in law an act of interference with the possession of land and is actionable in a civil court without proof of damage. A court order may be made prohibiting a repetition and, if the order is disobeyed, damages may be awarded.

If a trespasser refuses to leave property when requested to do so, under common law, they may lawfully be removed by the use of only such force as is necessary to eject them. A security officer employed by the owner of the land or premises concerned is the owner's agent and can exercise the powers of the owner.

In the majority of cases trespassers have quite innocent intentions and will leave immediately they are told they are trespassing. However, should their actions suggest a presence for a sinister purpose the police should be informed and, in the meantime, they should be kept under observation. If the area is one where research or other sensitive work is being carried out, the possibility of industrial espionage should not be overlooked.

With privatisation, security personnel may find themselves responsible for places to which the Official Secrets Act applies and under which certain indictable offences are committed by 'any person for any purpose prejudicial to the safety or the interests of the state' who does a variety of things, including approaching, inspecting, passing over, being in the neighbourhood of or entering any prohibited place. Such officer should ensure that they fully understand the instructions laid down for such contingencies and, of course, they should not allow their own inquisitiveness to make them act in a manner that might be misconstrued.

The name and address of trespassers who will not concern the police should be requested, but no further action is available if the information is refused.

Offences relating to trespassers under the Criminal Law Act 1977 are mainly concerned with squatters, but two provisions should be noted. It is an offence to use or threaten violence to gain entry without lawful authority into any premises where a person is opposed to the entry and the person's views are known to the intruder. A person might well be a guarding security officer. It should be noted that an owner whose premises have been taken over has to rely on civil action to get them back. The second offence is that of having entered as a trespasser and being in possession of a weapon of offence without authority or reasonable excuse.

Under certain circumstances there is a power of arrest for persons other than the police conferred under the Vagrancy Act 1824, which created the offence of 'being found on enclosed premises for an unlawful purpose', and a person other than the police may arrest a person found in or upon a building or in an enclosed yard or area for an unlawful purpose. The enclosure must be small and adjacent to a building, and the fact that it may have an open gate or archway does not negate the offence, but the purpose of being there must be one that can be shown to be unlawful. The time of day is immaterial. This power could well be used for persons found within a factory perimeter.

The Criminal Attempts Act 1981 created an offence of interfering with a motor vehicle, trailer or anything in or on it with intent to steal or drive it away without consent. Power of arrest under this legislation is restricted to the police, who will not have to prove which of the alternatives were intended – as opposed to an 'attempt' where the objective has to be specified. To be caught undoing the straps and connections of a lorry battery may be an offence of interfering, but in the absence of a feasible explanation, it could also be attempted theft of a battery and thus subject to an 'any person' power of arrest.

Criminal trespass

The Criminal Justice and Public Order Act 1994 created a number of criminal offences relating to trespassing on land, giving the police powers to remove two or more people who are trespassing on land where the occupier or his agent has asked them to leave.

Section 6(1): trespassing on land

> *If the senior police officer present reasonably believes that two or more persons are trespassing on land and they have a common purpose of residing there for any period and reasonable steps have been taken to ask them to leave by or on behalf of the occupier, and (a) any of those persons have caused damage to the land or property thereon or (b) any of those persons has used threatening, insulting words or behaviour, towards the occupier or his employee, his family or agent, or (c) those persons have six or more vehicles on the land he may direct them to leave the land and remove any vehicles or other property.*

If people lawfully on land become trespassers – that is, after they have been told to leave – the above direction can only be given if all other conditions as stated above are satisfied *after* the moment they became trespassers.

Section 61(4): failure to leave land as directed

It is an offence for a person knowing that direction to leave has been given to: (a) fail to leave land as soon as is reasonably practicable or (b) leave and return as a trespasser within three months of the date of the direction.

Section 61(5) and 62(1): police powers

These sections give a constable in uniform the power to arrest a person whom he or she reasonably suspects has failed to leave the land as directed or who has returned as a trespasser within three months. Also, constables may seize and remove any vehicle which they reasonably suspect belongs to or is in the possession or control of a person to whom the direction applies, who has, without reasonable excuse, failed to remove it or re-entered land with it as a trespasser within three months.

Aggravated trespass

Section 68 of the Criminal Justice and Public Order Act 1994 deals with an offence of aggravated trespass, where persons have entered land in the open air in order to disrupt, obstruct or deter people from carrying out any event or work. This is, for example, particularly applicable to security staff who are engaged in protecting areas of natural beauty earmarked for new roads, or those hired to prevent hunt saboteurs obstructing a foxhunt. Under Section 68:

It is an offence for a person to trespass on land in the open air and do there anything which is intended to (a) intimidate so as to deter, (b) obstruct or (c) disrupt persons engaged or about to engage in lawful activity on that or adjacent land in the open air.

Sections 68(4), 69(1) and 69(3): police powers

These sections give the senior police officer present the power to direct persons to leave the land, creates an offence of failing to do so as soon as is reasonably practicable, and gives a constable in uniform the power to arrest any person he or she reasonably suspects to be committing the offences.

INTIMIDATION OF PERSONS CONNECTED TO ANIMAL RESEARCH ORGANISATIONS

In recent years there has been increased intimidation directed towards the premises and employees of organisations involved in the use of animals for research purposes. Under Section 146 of the Serious Organised Crime and Police Act 2005:

> It is an offence for a person to threaten another person, that he, or someone else, will do a criminal act or a tortuous act which would lead to loss or damage, with the intention to cause the person threatened to do or not to do something which he is entitled to do or abstain from.

In essence, under this legislation an offence is committed if an owner or employee of an animal research establishment is threatened or intimidated in order to get them to stop what they are doing.

The offence is indictable, and therefore a power of arrest for persons other than the police is available, subject to the arrest conditions as discussed in Chapter 10.

COMPENSATION FOR INJURIES

This is an appropriate point at which to mention a sometimes controversial topic. A company's insurance policies may not contain any specific provision for compensating a security officer who is injured in preventing an attack on his employer's property. Such policies are normally designed to cover negligence claims. While *ex-gratia* payments may be authorised, the situation should be clarified before an incident occurs. Application forms and details of compensation for injury sustained from a 'reported-to-police' crime of violence can, however be obtained from the Criminal Injuries Compensation Board. Considerable delay must be anticipated in achieving a settlement, and it should be remembered that a court that convicts an offender can order compensation to be paid to the victim as part of the sentence.

10 Powers of Arrest

An arrest involves depriving someone of their liberty or restraining them so they are available to answer questions about an alleged crime that is an indictable offence. In order to arrest, it is not necessary to lay hands on a person; it is enough that they have been made aware by words or actions that they are under arrest and cannot go freely as they might wish.

ARREST BY A PERSON OTHER THAN A CONSTABLE

The right of a private person, which includes security officers, to arrest without warrant for an indictable offence is conferred by Section 24(A) of the Police and Criminal Evidence Act 1984, as amended by Section 110 of the Serious and Organised Crime and Police Act 2005. The powers conferred under the Act are as follows:

> 1. *Any person other than a constable may arrest without warrant anyone who is in the act of committing an indictable offence or anyone whom he has reasonable grounds for suspecting to be committing an indictable offence.*

> 2. *Where an indictable offence has been committed a person other than a constable may arrest without warrant anyone who is guilty of the offence or anyone whom he has reasonable grounds for suspecting to be guilty of it.*

A constable may arrest for *any* offence, but a person other than a constable is restricted to arresting for indictable offences only. Indictable offences are those that are triable at crown court (and include those that are triable *either* at a magistrates' court or a crown court). Examples of indictable offences include:

* murder and manslaughter
* rape

- serious assault
- possession or supply of unlawful drugs
- criminal damage
- theft, robbery, burglary and fraud offences
- possessing an offensive weapon
- going equipped to steal
- aggravated vehicle taking (where a vehicle is taken, then damaged)
- indecent exposure
- causing death by dangerous or careless driving.

The power of arrest is only exercisable if:

- the person making the arrest has reasonable grounds for believing that for any reasons mentioned in Section 110(4) of the Serious and Organised Crime and Police Act (see below) it is necessary to arrest the person in question; and
- it appears to the person making the arrest that it is not reasonably practicable for a constable to make the arrest instead.

Section 110(4)(a) to (d) sets out the reasons why it may be necessary to arrest the person in question and to prevent them leaving the scene. These are to prevent:

(a)   causing physical injury to himself or any other person;

(b)   suffering physical injury;

(c)   causing loss or damage to property; or

(d)   making off before a constable can assume responsibility for them.

It should be noted that the power uses 'reasonable grounds for believing' in relation to the arrest being necessary, which is a higher standard than reasonable grounds for suspecting. The person must have reasonable grounds to believe that the arrest is necessary to prevent one of the four reasons mentioned above, and that it appears to the person making the arrest that it is not reasonably practicable for a constable to make the arrest.

The legislation does infer that there will probably be some urgency to make the arrest, particularly where a constable is not present or where it may be some time before a constable arrives at the scene. It is reasonable to expect a person to make the arrest in order to prevent a person escaping the scene having committed an indictable offence.

Reasonable grounds for suspecting

Reasonable grounds for suspicion will depend very much on the circumstances in each case, but there must be some objective basis for that suspicion based on facts and information.

'Reasonable' means that grounds must be based on objective facts that another person could evaluate, such as:

- the person's behaviour;
- the time and place where the person is;
- any property they are carrying.

A good test of whether the arresting person has reasonable grounds to suspect is whether an independent person would come to the same conclusion when presented with all the facts.

Reasonable grounds for believing

Again, there can never be a hard and fast definition, and grounds for believing will depend on the circumstances of each case. However, 'grounds for believing' is a stronger standard than simply suspecting something, and it would need to be supported by stronger objective facts.

INFORMATION TO BE GIVEN UPON ARREST

At the time of the arrest the arrested person must be cautioned and told that they are under arrest and the grounds for the arrest, including the reason and the indictable offence for which they have been arrested. The caution must be learned by the security officer and administered as follows:

> *You do not have to say anything, but it may harm your defence if you do not mention when questioned something which you later rely on in court. Anything you do say will be given in evidence.*

It is important at this stage that the reply of the arrested person is noted, and written down as soon as possible, and that the police are told of the reply when they arrive.

USE OF FORCE

Should a person resist arrest, a reasonable amount of force may be used in order to carry out the arrest. Section 3(1) of the Criminal Law Act 1967 says that any person may use such force as is 'reasonable' in the circumstances in order to (a) prevent a crime, (b) detain or assist in the detention of an offender or suspected offender or (c) detain or assist in the detention of a person unlawfully at large. Reasonable force may be used to:

- defend oneself
- defend others
- protect property
- make an arrest.

The key watchword to be observed when exercising force is reasonable. The interpretation of reasonable force defends on a number of factors. These include:

- the gravity of the crime that the person was trying to prevent;
- whether it was possible to prevent the crime by non-violent means;
- whether the person exercising force was ready to try non-violent means first;
- the relative strengths of the parties involved.

If there are grounds for believing that a person used unreasonable force, he or she could be charged with an offence of assault, or murder or manslaughter if the person subjected to the force dies. To convict a person who has used force in order to prevent a crime, detain a person or in self-defence, a court must be satisfied that no reasonable person in a similar position would have considered the use of such force justified.

PRECAUTIONS AFTER ARREST

Once a suspect has been placed under arrest, someone must remain with that person at all times until the arrival of the police. If a female has been arrested, a female member of staff must be present. It is at this time that vital evidence of an offence can be lost, usually because the suspect has been allowed to distract the arresting officer by using amiable chatter or by them otherwise being persuaded to relax vigilance.

Be aware of the risk that items likely to prove the commission of an offence may be disposed of between the time of arrest and the police arrival. If there is a request to use a toilet, then the detained person must be escorted. The toilet must be searched before and after the detained person has used it. If the suspect has been transported in a car, it must be searched immediately afterwards. Also, vigilance must be maintained so that the detained person does not harm themselves. In summary, vigilance is necessary to:

- prevent the loss of vital evidence;
- prevent the detained person causing an injury to themselves;
- prevent the detained person from causing injury to other people.

Once a person has been arrested there is a legal obligation to hand over the detained person into police custody as soon as possible.

QUESTIONING AFTER ARREST

If it is the policy of the company to involve the police when a criminal offence has been identified and a person arrested, the suspect (detained person) must not be questioned about the alleged offence by security personnel before the police arrive. It is the job of the police to question the suspect with regard to the statutory rights the detained person has under the Police and Criminal Evidence Act 1984 (PACE). Any prior questioning without regard to PACE may not be admissible as evidence and may obstruct any further enquiries the police might wish to make into the alleged crime.

If the matter is one that is to be dealt with in-house, following the practices of PACE may not be necessary, but it may be advisable to allow the person the right to have someone informed of their predicament or someone present if they are to be questioned about the matter. An over-zealous interview might lead to problems should there be a claim for unfair dismissal at an industrial tribunal.

UNLAWFUL ARREST

The risk of a claim for damages if a mistaken arrest is made is often raised as a deterrent to those who wish to take advantages of their lawful powers in the prevention of crime or to detain offenders. That contingency must be put into perspective. Actions in the civil courts for damages due to an unlawful arrest are extremely rare, taking into consideration the total number of arrests made for every sort of offence and for those offences that are not brought to justice.

If there are reasonable grounds for believing or suspecting that an arrested person is responsible for an indictable offence, then the arresting officer has nothing to fear. That officer's actions in detaining the person are perfectly legal even if subsequent enquiries show that the person was not the offender, or indeed that an offence was not committed.

Courts dealing with claims for damages are sympathetic towards arresting officers who honestly believed they were acting in accordance with the law and *without malice*, providing the grounds for the arrest were reasonable.

11 Police Procedure Following Private Arrest

When police assistance is requested following an arrest by a person other than the police, the police officer attending will ask to be told the facts of the case and the evidence available that indicates that the arrested person has committed an offence. This must take place in the presence and hearing of the arrested person.

BASIC POLICE REQUIREMENTS

Police procedures may differ from one force to another, but the basic actions and requirements are the same. The person responsible for arresting the suspect must tell the police officer what they saw, what they said to the suspect and the suspect's reply. Also, at this time the person who made the arrest will indicate whether any property that is the subject of the alleged offence has been recovered, and, if it has, the property must be formally identified to the police in the presence of the arrested person.

The police officer will then ask the suspect if he or she wishes to comment on what the arresting person has said. The police officer will then caution the detained person stating that they do not have to say anything, but that it may harm their defence if they do not mention when questioned something which they later rely on in court, and that anything they do say may be given in evidence. If the evidence presented to the police officer is considered to present a prima facie case against the detained person, the police officer may arrest that person to be detained at a police station.

Once at the police station the detained person is taken before the custody officer. The arresting police officer will outline the facts of the case and the reasons for arrest to the custody officer. This is done in the presence and hearing of the detained person. Before accepting the person into custody, the custody officer must be satisfied that an offence has been committed and that there are reasonable grounds for suspecting that the detained person is responsible. Once the detained person has been accepted into custody, the custody officer will explain the rights that the person has while in detention. These rights are:

- the right to speak to an independent solicitor free of charge;
- the right to have someone told of the arrest;
- the right to consult a copy of the codes of practice covering police powers and procedures.

Once all enquiries are complete, the offence is written out on a charge sheet and the detained person is cautioned and charged with the alleged offence. When other administrative procedures are complete, the accused is usually released on bail to appear at the magistrates' court on a later date, unless the offence is of a very serious nature, or the background and history of the detained person suggests that bail is either not appropriate (where a remand in custody will be applied for) or that the person is not likely to appear at court if given bail.

Where a person has been arrested for an offence or reported for summons there are several possible outcomes. These include:

- the issue of a fixed penalty notice if, in the case of theft, the property has been recovered and the value of the property is below a certain amount;
- no further action;
- informal warning;
- verbal caution by a senior police officer;
- prosecution.

The outcomes are influenced by a number of factors including:

- the quality of the evidence;
- the views of the complainant in the case;
- any previous convictions or cautions recorded against the detained person;
- whether a prosecution is in the public interest.

BAIL

Where a person has been taken into custody after an arrest made by a person other than a police officer, such as a security officer, the accused must be taken to a police station as soon as possible after the arrest unless:

- the presence of that person is necessary elsewhere in order to carry out investigations that are required immediately;
- the accused is immediately released on bail by the police officer – a process known as street bail;
- the accused is released by the police officer, who is satisfied that there are no grounds for keeping them under arrest.

Where an accused has been taken to a police station, bail may be granted by the police or by a court, and conditions may be attached to that bail restricting the movements of the bailed person or preventing them interfering with witnesses or entering a certain town or street. Also, in serious cases a court allowing bail may require the accused person to provide sureties, where people associated with the accused will agree to pay the court a certain sum of money should the accused not appear at court at the given time and date. In considering whether to grant bail or not, the police and courts will take into account the following:

- the circumstances and seriousness of the offence charged;
- the nature and scale of any enquiries still to be made;
- any previous convictions of the accused;
- the level of further threat to the complainant;
- whether other people are involved and whether arrested or not;
- any doubts about the accused person surrendering to bail;
- the likelihood of the accused person committing offences while on bail;
- the likelihood of the accused interfering with witnesses or obstructing justice;
- whether or not the accused has a fixed abode.

If there is a likelihood that any of these conditions cannot be met, the police may apply to the courts for the accused person to be remanded in custody. However, most arrested people will be granted bail. This may cause embarrassment if the accused person is an employee, the alleged crime has been committed against the employer, and the employee re-presents themselves for work. If a person attends work in such circumstances, the human resources department or its equivalent must be informed before the person is allowed on to the premises. Disciplinary proceedings may commence at once before any decision is taken by the police or the Crown Prosecution Service on whether to prosecute the accused person; dismissal may be fair regardless of the result of court proceedings or action short of prosecution.

WITNESS STATEMENTS

Statements or proofs of evidence from witnesses are taken down in writing by the police. Each page is signed by the witness. These statements are the basis on which the decision to caution or charge the accused person will be taken or whether court proceedings will be commenced. It is necessary that a key witness statement – that is, a written statement from a person who is providing significant evidence that will prove the offence – is obtained before the accused person is charged by the police; this might involve taking such a statement shortly after a person has been arrested.

Since the passing of the Criminal Justice Act 1967, evidence can be adduced at court by reading from written statements of witnesses subject to certain conditions. This requires the editing of the statement in order to remove hearsay and other passages that would not be admissible if the witness were to give evidence orally. Both the original and any subsequent statements that have been edited must be carefully checked by the maker to ensure that their contents coincide with the evidence the witness is competent to give.

Although a written statement may be admissible on a court's own motion or on the application of any party to the proceedings, the person making it may be required to attend court and give evidence.

If a witness wilfully includes in a statement anything that is known to be false, under the Act that person is liable to prosecution. At court, a witness is entitled to refresh their memory by reading the statement made to the police before giving evidence.

PROPERTY EXHIBITS

Any property that is the subject of proceedings may be retained by the police, but it is usual practice for it to be retained by the owner or the person who may be required to present it as evidence at court. It is usual, also, for the property to be retained once a person has been convicted until after the time allowed for an appeal against conviction has passed.

RETURN OF STOLEN PROPERTY

Section 28 of the Theft Act 1968 provides the authority by which stolen goods are returned by a court to their owners.

Where a person is convicted of any offence relating to the theft, the court may order any person having possession or control of the goods to return them to the owner. The application for this action is normally made by the police, unless there are any complications; some police forces insist on the complainant's presence.

The stolen property may have been converted by the thief into some other form of goods. In this case, when the thief is convicted, the owner of the original goods or his authorised agent can apply to the court for an order that a sum equivalent to their value should be paid by the accused in compensation. If no application is made for compensation at the time of the court proceedings, a civil action may be the only way to secure restitution.

COMPENSATION

Where an individual or organisation has suffered loss through a criminal act, in the interest of their insurers or shareholders, and as a deterrent against a possible recurrence, they should consider how best to obtain compensation from any person subsequently convicted of the offence. Civil proceedings for compensation may be expensive, unpredictable in outcome and extremely long-winded, but a potential remedy is vested in the power of the court that convicts the culprit.

The Powers of Criminal Courts Act 1973 (Section 35) empowers a convicting court, in addition to dealing with the offender in any other way, on application or otherwise, to make an order requiring the convicted person to pay compensation for any personal injury, loss or damage resulting from their offence, or any other offence which the accused has had taken into consideration by the court in determining sentence. 'Offence' is not restricted to theft. It is equally applicable to property damage, physical injury and other sources of loss – for example, the financial loss occasioned after a 'bomb hoax' telephone call. There are exclusions, with offences under the Road Traffic Acts being the main ones, although a vehicle damaged during the commission of a Theft Act offence (taking and driving away) could be the subject of a claim.

The power is one that the court *may* use. Compensation is not automatic, nor will it be awarded if the circumstances are complicated.

Victims of crime are usually given a court compensation application form by the police investigating officer, and where compensation is required, this form should be completed and sent directly to the court. Security officers giving a statement should insist on including that their employer wishes the court to exercise its powers to make a compensation award. This is all the more important as it may induce the Crown Prosecution Service to press proceedings when otherwise a contentious decision not to do so might have been made, thereby depriving the complainant of the right to a compensation award.

12 Searching

No private person, which includes a security officer, has the right to search any person, their property or vehicle unless it is with the consent of the person being searched. The agreement of an employee to a clause in the company's conditions of employment requiring that they submit to a personal search as a preventive measure to theft does not remove the necessity to obtain consent to the search first. It is not a criminal offence to fail to submit to a search.

A refusal to be searched is not in itself grounds for suspicion that a crime has been committed or for detaining or attempting to detain a person, unless, allied to the refusal is other credible evidence that the person has, or is suspected of having, stolen property in their possession. In these latter circumstances, the security professional would have reasonable grounds for believing that the person was in the act of committing an indictable offence and would have the power to lawfully arrest that person and detain them until the police arrived (see Chapter 10).

The police have statutory powers to search under the Police and Criminal Evidence Act 1984, and this requires them to conform to strict codes of practice when doing so.

EMPLOYER'S RIGHT TO SEARCH

It is sometimes the practice in manufacturing workplaces – particularly where raw materials or finished products are an attractive commodity to the employee and can be secreted on the person – for the conditions of employment to include a clause concerning personal searching. This may also apply to retail or other establishments where there is obvious temptation and opportunity but where searching may be restricted to bags, parcels and the like. When an employee accepts an offer of employment under the conditions, a contract has been made between employee and employer. Thereafter, if the employee fails to comply with the conditions, the contract is broken, rendering the employee liable to disciplinary action, which could result in dismissal.

The words of the search clause may differ from company to company, but its essentials are the same. It is important that the security officer knows the contents of all the employer's regulations.

SEARCH METHOD

The extent and thoroughness of personal searching depends on the type of property likely to be concealed. The searching of employees engaged in the handling of precious stones, for example, cannot be carried out effectively unless they are required to strip to the skin. The same may be called for where valuable rare metals are involved, though hand-held or 'doorway'-type metal detectors may be more appropriate in these circumstances. If such equipment is used, even minor responses must be clarified before exit is allowed. If the product is foodstuffs, however, it might be sufficient to inspect bags or packages carried and to run the hands lightly over the outside of the employee's clothing.

The determined thief will conceal property wherever possible. The person conducting the search must keep an open mind, and this will depend very much on the size of the article. A large piece of property cannot be concealed in a small place.

SEARCHING CONTRACTORS' VEHICLES AND STAFF

If an agreement has been made with contractors carrying out work on the premises under which their employees and the employees of subcontractors become subject of the same conditions respecting safety, no smoking rules and security as the company's employees, then the opportunity to carry out searches of both vehicles and employees must not be neglected. Any objections to complying with searching must be reported to the person's employer and the security officer's own superiors.

SEARCHING PROCEDURE

Searches at the exit of premises are more effective if a small group of employees are chosen and they are searched one by one rather than making individual selections as employees leave. The fact of searches being made will soon become known to later leavers, who, if they are carrying anything stolen, will try to dispose of the property. The operation becomes more effective therefore if a security officer stands in a position to observe any such attempts at disposal while the searching is being carried out by others.

The main point to be considered before any search is conducted is that a search is personally intrusive and may impinge on rights to respect and privacy under the Human Rights Act. The following basic procedures are recommended when people have consented to a search:

- A woman must only be searched by a woman.

- If the person to be searched wishes it to be conducted out of the view of other people, the request should be granted.

- Do not treat searching as an operation that is anything out of the ordinary.

- Make selections at random, but try to avoid searching the same individual regularly. This might cause the person to believe that he or she is being singled out unfairly and may lead to complaints.

- If there is a positive suspect who needs to be included, do so in a manner that will not raise suspicion of special selection. This might point to the person who has provided the information on which the search is based.

- Unless a really detailed physical search is required, as might occur with jewellery or rare metals, there is no reason why searching should not be carried out openly with two or three employees there at the same time. Apart from giving the impression of routine, this will also show that everything is being done openly and fairly. If an employee requests privacy, agree to that privilege.

- The employee should be asked to step inside the security office for a routine search. If the employee does not appear to understand the reasons for the search or the procedure, the security officer must explain fully and indicate to the employee that acquiescence to searching is included in the conditions of employment. This should be done quietly and politely without too formal an attitude.

- If a person to be searched wishes to have a friend present at the time, this should be allowed.

- In the event of refusal to be searched, it must be pointed out that this is a breach of an employment condition and that the refusal could result in disciplinary action. The reason for the refusal must be recorded and entered into the search register and the full details of the person and the circumstances reported to senior management.

- If there has been reliable information that stolen property is in the possession of a person refusing to be searched, the action taken will depend on the circumstances because the refusal may add credence to the information. Provided there are reasonable grounds for believing that stolen property is in the possession of the person refusing to be searched, that person may be lawfully arrested and the police notified. People cannot be detained against their will without lawful arrest.

- Before searching, employees *must* be asked if there is any property that does not belong to them in their possession and must be given the opportunity to produce such an item. If property is produced, the employee must be given the opportunity to explain whether the property is stolen, possessed as purchased, or authorised. The latter two explanations must be checked immediately.

- If a search is permitted, it must be carried out quickly and thoroughly to the extent necessitated by the size of the goods likely to have been stolen.

- If the result of the search is negative, thank the person, ask for their signature in the search register and let them leave immediately. The date and time of the search should be entered into the register along with the signature of the searching officer and any comments made by employees about the conduct of the search.

- If articles are produced or found upon an employee, and they have been identified as belonging to the company, the employer's regulations and instructions for theft should be implemented.

SEARCH AFTER ARREST

When a person is taken into police custody, it is a practice approved by law that they are personally searched. However, after arrest by a person other than a police officer and before police arrival, the detained person must be asked to empty the contents of any pockets or baggage, although they have the right to refuse. Refusal to empty pockets and baggage does not give the security officer the right to search. The request to empty pockets and baggage must be made in order to:

- remove any weapon or other articles that could be used to cause injury to themselves or others;

- find and preserve evidence of an offence.

The searching of people is a very emotive subject. Every precaution must be taken to ensure the human rights and dignity of the person being searched. With increasing terrorism, people have come to expect the need for searches to be carried out, particularly when gaining entrance to public buildings, airports and the like. It must, however, be borne in mind that the consent of the person is still required before a search can be carried out. There is no excuse for the security officer to be offhand or impolite at the expense of someone who has reservations about being searched. Courtesy and respect are the watchwords at all times.

13 Investigation and Questioning

In dealing with both suspected persons and genuine witnesses, the amount of truthful information that can be obtained is determined by the approach of the questioner, who must vary technique in accordance with the personality of the individual being spoken to. Formality, sympathy, bonhomie, incredulity and even a degree of flattery may be needed to persuade a witness to divulge information. It must always be remembered that the object of all questioning is to ascertain the truth, no matter how inconvenient or distasteful it may be, and not to induce a pattern of deceit.

QUESTIONING SUSPECTED PERSONS

Ideally, if there is an allegation that a criminal offence has taken place, the questioning of suspected persons should be left to the police. However, if it has been decided by management that the allegation is to be dealt with internally, this does not diminish the rights of the suspect to seek legal advice or to have someone present during an interview. Any interview conducted with a suspect must take place within parameters set by the Police and Criminal Evidence Act 1984 (PACE).

PACE codes of practice for questioning suspects

These codes are designed to ensure absolute fairness to suspects, and that any statements or answers to questions that may be tendered in subsequent evidence are made voluntarily and were not obtained by oppressive means, false promises, deception or in any other manner that renders them unreliable.

PACE and its codes of practice make it mandatory for evidence obtained contrary to their provisions to be excluded. Section 67(9) of the Act says:

Persons other than police officers who are charged with the duty of investigating offences or charging offenders shall, in the discharge of their duty, have regard to the relevant provisions of a code issued under the Act.

A Home Office dictum says that security officers do not come within the purview of Section 67 but that 'they should have regard to the standards, so far as in common sense they are applicable to the work they do'. Judges had previously said that store detectives definitely did have to comply with the code rules. Pending any new judicial decisions based upon the Act, common sense dictates that security officers dealing with their employers' staff, or with intruders on the premises they have a duty to guard, and store detectives involved with shoplifters, should conform to the codes.

The most important point for a security officer is that of administering a caution to a suspect to ensure that what is subsequently said is admissible in evidence; if an arrest is made the caution must be given. However, if questioning is needed to establish guilt when there are grounds to believe a person has committed an offence, that person must be cautioned before any questions or further questions are asked. The caution, although mentioned before, is worth repeating. It reads:

You do not have to say anything, but it may harm your defence if you do not mention when questioned something which you later rely on in court. Anything you do say will be given in evidence.

The caution is not necessary when questions are asked for any purpose unconnected with possible charges, such as that of obtaining identity, address, responsibility of ownership and so on.

There are detailed rules about taking written statements from detained persons or suspects and a security officer would be well advised not to do this unless there are special instructions.

In writing notes on an arrest, a security officer should show, among other details, the point at which the caution was given and the questions and answers that are pertinent should be recorded verbatim. The penalty for non-compliance is non-admissibility, and if proceedings rest on admissions or answers given then a guilty person can go free.

From a security officer's point of view, the questioning of a suspect should be kept to a minimum consistent with establishing that no mistake has been made and that the individual has been given every opportunity to explain the circumstances. If the facts speak for themselves, the less said the better.

PACE does not apply in Scotland, nor is there anything comparable to Section 67(9); it has been said that when police suspicion has centred on a person to the extent that a charge is likely to be made, further interrogation becomes dangerous. Security officers in Scotland should not administer a caution and should cease questioning as would the police. If questioning is carried to the point of extracting a confession, the evidence will almost certainly be excluded.

INDUSTRIAL COURT APPLICATION

It was held by an industrial appeals tribunal (in *Morley's of Brixton Ltd.* v *Minott* 1982) that the then Judges' Rules on interviewing suspects (now replaced by a PACE code of practice) were not binding in civil litigation; they were for the protection of an individual from criminal conviction, so that while the circumstances might affect the weight given to an admission, it would not be excluded in evidence. In this case, the accused claimed that there had been an implication that there would be no dismissal from work if an admission were made; he confessed and was then dismissed. The court said that encouragement to 'come clean' in disciplinary enquires was not improper conduct and that the import of such technicalities as the Judges' Rules would make the life of the employer impossible.

Although this ruling was made before the introduction of PACE, it has held good since and has been confirmed by rulings that make it obvious that the industrial courts do not intend themselves to be bound by the technicalities of the Act.

INTERVIEWS

Planning interviews

The object of an interview is to obtain the truth of the matter under investigation. Good planning and preparation is essential. When planning an interview, the interviewer must:

- understand the purpose of the interview;
- define the aims and objectives of the interview;
- recognise and understand the points necessary to prove the offence;
- analyse the evidence available;

- assess what evidence is needed and where it can be obtained;
- understand PACE and the corresponding codes of practice.

Preparing for the interview

In preparing for an interview the following should be considered:

- where the interview is to take place;
- who is to conduct the interview and who else should be present;
- when to carry out the interview;
- reducing any possible distractions;
- having any documentary evidence or exhibits available.

Manner and form of questioning

Try to acquire the following characteristics when questioning suspects and witnesses:

- Be tactful and avoid causing resentment or friction.
- Be patient and do not show any signs of boredom.
- Be a good listener and try to create confidence. Encourage the witness to talk confidently.
- Do not interrupt, except to get the conversation back to the point or to cut short a repetitive explanation.
- Do not ridicule or rebuke the speaker or show annoyance.
- Do not make threats under any circumstances, either verbally or physically, irrespective of the behaviour of the other person.
- Do not make promises or offer any inducements. Do not use any deceit to obtain answers.
- Be agreeable and straightforward in your approach, which should accord with the treatment you would expect if roles were reversed.
- Do not be diverted from your objective by a display of verbal aggression from the person to whom you are speaking.
- Be persistent until you find out what you want to know and are satisfied that it is a true version. Ignore any display of impatience by the other party.

The actual form of questioning should follow similar basic principles:

- Phrase questions clearly and in a language the listener thoroughly understands.

- Do not ask questions that are in any way ambiguous or could lead the listener to think an effort is being made to trick them.

- Where ambiguous answers are given, put further questions with the express purpose of ensuring there is no misunderstanding on either side.

- Ask questions methodically to avoid omitting any material matters and to ensure that no gaps are left during which an untruthful witness could collect their thoughts.

- Ask questions quietly but clearly with a display of interest in the forthcoming answer.

- Avoid leading questions such as those that can be answered by a plain yes or no.

TAKING WITNESS STATEMENTS

If a person has information to convey, do not promptly produce a notebook or sheet of paper, sit down and start writing. This can cause a witness to close up almost completely; it is better to break down barriers of reserve and at the same time get a clear picture of what has happened before committing anything to paper. A more readable, coherent and comprehensive statement will result, and greater cooperation will be forthcoming from the witness.

One style of statement taking is the cognitive approach, which can be summarised as follows:

- Encourage the witness to ask questions at any time, rather than to have doubts or uncertainties.

- Explain what you require of the witness – for example, that they will have to describe what they have seen or what they have suffered and that this will involve them 'reliving' the incident.

- Ask them to speak slowly as this will allow for notes to be taken.

- Put the witness at ease. This will assist recall.

- Ask the witness to concentrate. This will assist with the recall of the incident and result in better information.

- Explain to the witness that initially you will let them do all the talking so that they can exhaust their memory of the incident before you speak to them again.

- Explain to the witness that the questions asked will allow them to speak again. Reassure the witness that you are listening to every word spoken.

Now is the time to make a positive start on the statement. The statement itself should not be written yet, but notes should be taken throughout to aid its taking. Ask the witness to recall everything they can about the incident. Ask them not to edit anything out. What they consider to be unimportant may be a vital piece of evidence. Let the witness control the flow of information because, at this time, the role of the interviewer is to listen.

It is also important that the emotions of the witness are considered. It must be remembered that the event they are trying to recall may have been a traumatic one and therefore the interviewer must be prepared to deal with any possible distress the witness may have. Emotions may have to be dealt with before the interview can continue.

The interviewer must not interrupt the witness as this may cause information to be lost. Wait until the witness has finished before raising any points. If a witness pauses, allow the pause to continue because interrupting it may deflect them from what they are trying to recall. Interrupting can hinder the recall process and hinder accuracy.

Once the witness has finished with the recall and notes have been taken to assist with the preparation of the statement, ask the witness to go through the incident once again, perhaps this time starting from the end of the incident. The more this is done, the more the witness will remember. When the statement appears complete, the interviewer can now ask probing questions in order to clear up any ambiguity. Differences in detail must be cleared up at this time and questions may assist the witness to recall matters not previously mentioned.

Once the witness's memory has been exhausted through the use of free recall and open questions, the information given can now be reviewed. This is useful for two reasons: (a) it may prompt the witness to give more information; and (b) it can allow the interviewer to check that every detail has been noted.

Finally, the statement can be written chronologically with the aid of the notes taken. It must be preceded by the full name and address and status of the maker, with an indication of their age. Once completed, the maker should read the statement so that any alterations and additions can be made, and then it must be signed.

14 Notebooks and Reports

A notebook is an essential tool for security officers. The reasons for keeping notebooks are as follows;

- To provide a permanent personal record of hours of duty and work performed.
- For the convenient and efficient recording of instructions, messages and incidents during the course of duty.
- To provide a source of recall and reference to any details arising from any incident or message that may require the compilation of a written statement or report.
- To record matters that cannot safely be entrusted to memory.
- As a source of confirmation for evidence given in court, particularly in respect of conversations that are material to proceedings.
- As a source of recall of facts relevant to the institution of internal disciplinary proceedings.

RULES FOR KEEPING NOTEBOOKS

These rules reflect the fact that a notebook must be clearly acceptable as a correct record. Also, remember that where criminal proceedings are instituted, a notebook entry giving a first description of an incident or descriptions of suspected offenders or details of any conversation held with suspects may be a document that is disclosable to the defence under the Criminal Procedure and Investigations Act 1996. It is therefore necessary that all entries are recorded properly, with clear regard to the following rules:

- Enter the date of issue and the name of the owner inside the front cover before using the notebook.
- Make all entries in black permanent ink.

- Make all entries in a chronological sequence.

- Make an entry for each working day, showing the date and times of commencement and termination of duty, even if nothing worthy of note occurs.

- Make entries at the time, or as soon as possible after, an incident has occurred.

- Do not erase anything.

- Do not tear pages out. If alterations are necessary cross out the entry so that it remains legible.

- Do not make additions between lines.

- Initial any alterations that are made, particularly relating to entries that may be referred to in court proceedings.

- Do not make jottings on any part of the notebook. Enter everything in the proper place, no matter how roughly.

ESSENTIAL MATTERS TO INCLUDE IN NOTEBOOKS

Every entry must be fully written up with all relevant details; this will enable security officers to carry out their duties properly. The following are typical examples of the information required:

- Instructions given at the time of commencement of duty.

- Details of any report of a crime or a complaint, including the name and address and works details of the complainant, the date, time and location of the incident, the full description of any property missing, the details of any witnesses to the loss or incident, and the time the report was made and details of any subsequent action taken.

- In the case of an arrest: the time, date, place and circumstances of the arrest, together with the name, age, address and works particulars (if an employee) of the detained person and details of the detained person's replies when arrested. The questions asked and any replies given must be recorded in direct speech and, if the official caution was used, the time that this was administered should be noted.

- For reports of lost and found property when taken other than at the security office or gatehouse: the date, time and place of the loss or find, together with a full description of the items concerned and the name, address and works particulars of the loser/finder. If the property is handed to a patrolling officer, the finder should sign the entry in the officer's notebook and, should the property be claimed by the finder before it is entered into the property store, the person claiming it should sign the notebook giving details of their name, address, works number and so on.

- Notes of accidents reported or seen.

- Details of fires located or reported.

USE IN COURT PROCEEDINGS

When giving evidence in court, notebooks should not generally be referred to unless it is necessary in the interests of accuracy to do so. For example, it is possible to recall the action connected with an arrest without reading or quoting from the narrative in a notebook, but a witness cannot be expected to remember the precise content of a conversation or a list of property after some time has elapsed.

The permission of the magistrates or judge is required before a notebook may be referred to during court proceedings. When it is referred to it should be produced quite openly where the whole court can see it. How the book is kept may be queried in order to establish whether it can be regarded as a reliable record, and the defence and the magistrates or judge have a right to inspect it.

REPORTS

All facts about incidents that justify reporting should be committed to paper at the earliest opportunity so as to preclude possible embarrassment to management or colleagues who may be questioned on matters about which they are uninformed. A brief interim note serves this purpose if the enquiry or action is not complete.

The object is to convey full, accurate and unambiguous information. The amount of detail and explanation needed is determined by the known familiarity of the recipient with the matter being reported on. No padding should be inserted to try to impress the reader with the thoroughness, efficiency and enthusiasm of the writer. The essential rules to follow are:

- Make the report as soon as possible and amplify it later if necessary.

- Indicate clearly for whom the report is intended.

- Indicate the contents with a brief, explanatory heading.
- Be clear, brief and to the point.
- Use plain, unambiguous language.
- Limit technical phraseology to those who will understand it.
- Do not use slang.
- Do not include personal opinion unless it is asked for or it is important to the report and is based on sound fact.
- For minor incidents that occur regularly, prepare and use a pro forma to save time in preparation and reading.

The persons for whom a report is intended should be listed on the first sheet, preferably at the top left side. Where individuals are expected to take some action in respect of the contents or have a supervisory responsibility over the writer, the report should be addressed to them, with copies for those other persons of appropriate status and departmental involvement in the incident.

Undercirculate rather than overcirculate security reports, especially where they are of a confidential nature. Clearly mark such reports 'Confidential' on the top and also on the sealed envelope, together with the name of the person who is to receive it. Reports must also be marked 'personal' to ensure that they are not opened by anyone other than the intended recipient. The onus of deciding restrictions on circulation rests with the originator, and if a recipient decides to extend it this is their responsibility.

Matters that may lead to disciplinary action against an employee should immediately be notified verbally to the appropriate manager, but must be confirmed as soon as possible by written report. Care must be taken that such reports are impartial and unbiased; if the allegations lead to dismissal and the full appeal procedure ensues, the contents of the report will be scrutinised for any sign of unfairness or exaggeration.

15 Evidence and Court Procedure

Anyone concerned with the investigation of an offence against the criminal law, or preparing for a prosecution, must know what would be acceptable to a court as evidence and what would be rejected. Where an enquiry reveals a breach of company rules the same principles should be adopted so that disciplinary action is not taken without justification; it must afterwards be able to stand critical examination by a third party.

LAW OF EVIDENCE

This determines, first, what facts may be proved in order to ascertain the innocence or guilt of the accused person and, secondly, how and by whom those facts may be proved. The word 'evidence' means the facts, testimony and documents that may legally be adduced in order to ascertain the fact under enquiry.

Direct evidence

Evidence is direct when it immediately establishes the very fact sought to be proved. This type of evidence is normally what a witness saw or heard connecting the accused directly with the offence.

Circumstantial evidence

Evidence is circumstantial when it establishes other facts so relevant to or connected with the fact to be proved that they support an inference or presumption of its existence. For example, if A was seen in a cloakroom by B to put her hands into the pocket of a coat which was not hers and take out some money, later proved to have been stolen, what B could say would be *direct evidence*. If, however, B saw A standing beside the coat from which money was later reported stolen and A was unable to account for the possession of a similar amount of money to that stolen, and denied being present in the cloakroom at the relevant time, what B could say would be *circumstantial evidence*. In association with the other evidence of finding the money in A's possession, and what the person had to say, that might help to prove any guilt.

Hearsay evidence

Evidence is hearsay when a witness cannot give direct evidence of a fact; for example, if B, who saw A steal the money, tells C what was seen, C's evidence of what he was told is hearsay and cannot be given in court. The evidence can be given only by B.

Another example is where a document has to be produced to prove a fact in a prosecution. The document can be produced only by the person who prepared it. For instance, the fraudulent addition of figures on a document would require evidence from the actual clerk who wrote the original figures and who would say that since he did so they have been altered by the addition of other figures falsifying them. In certain cases, however, books and records kept by a company in the routine course of its business can be produced by someone other than the person who has written them.

Corroboration

This, broadly speaking, is evidence that confirms some other material evidence that the accused is guilty of the crime committed. It is considered desirable under common law that there should be corroboration of the evidence of three types of witness: accomplices, sexual complainants and children.

Opinion

Ordinary witnesses must give evidence of the facts within their knowledge and recollection and not of their opinions. It is for a court to draw opinions from what the witness has to say. Experts in particular fields, such as medicine, art or foreign law, may be called upon to give authoritative opinions, and their competency to do so may be challenged.

DISCLOSURE OF EVIDENCE

A code of practice has been issued under the Criminal Procedure and Investigations Act 1996 relating to the disclosure of evidence in criminal cases. A criminal investigation is an investigation carried out by a police officer. The code sets out the manner in which police officers are to record, retain and reveal to the prosecutor material obtained in a criminal investigation that may be relevant to the investigation and related matters. 'Material' can be of any kind, including objects that are obtained during the course of a criminal investigation, and material may be relevant to an investigation if it appears to the police investigator that it has some bearing on any offence under investigation or any person being investigated.

Implications for the security officer

Where a security officer is involved in a criminal incident in which the police are required to investigate, any documents or exhibits collected or made by the security officer may become disclosable and of importance to the investigation. Therefore, scribbled notes, notebook entries and related reports may be disclosable evidence.

Security officers should therefore make accurate records of incidents that are likely to be the basis of a criminal investigation and retain any material, such as written notes, that may be of interest to the police. Such material should be sealed in envelopes and locked away until the police have assessed its use in the investigation.

EXHIBITS

These are tangible objects produced in court that go towards proving the guilt and sometimes the innocence of the accused person. They are evidence in themselves, but they have to be produced in court by witnesses who speak of how and when they were found and explain their connection with the accused.

An exhibit can be a weapon alleged to have been used to cause injury that is the subject of a charge, the hair of an injured person deposited on such a weapon that is found in the possession of the accused, fibres found on clothing that will connect an accused to a crime, the tape recorded

interview of the accused, or (most commonly) property concerned in a charge of theft, subsequently recovered in whole or in part.

In the investigation of a serious crime, a security officer should leave the collection and handling of exhibits to the police, providing they can be safely preserved at the scene. The more an exhibit is handled, the easier it is to challenge the validity of the exhibit as evidence. Exhibits should be treated with care to avoid confusing fingerprint or forensic evidence, and they should be placed in a plastic bag or clean container labelled to show the time, place, date and details of the finder, before being lodged in a safe place until collection. In cases of serious crime, it is better that the security officer preserves the scene with the exhibits intact than to attempt to recover them. Always be guided by the advice of the police on first contact.

Sound and video recordings are now acceptable in evidence, supporting the use of CCTV. Documents in the form of computer printouts and photographs are also accepted in evidence. However, the validity of such evidence has to be proved by a competent witness.

MODE OF TRIAL

Offences fall into three categories (as regards persons who have attained the age of 17):

1. Triable only summarily, that is by magistrates at the magistrates' court.

2. Triable only on indictment at the crown court.

3. Triable either way (the magistrates have the discretion to try or commit the matter to the crown court having regard to the gravity of the offence and any representations made to them by the prosecutor or the accused).

In (3) the accused will be warned, if the case is to be dealt with summarily, that if found guilty the magistrates have the power to commit to the crown court for sentence should the character and antecedents of the accused lead them to believe that a penalty beyond their powers is called for.

PROCEDURE IN COURT

Examination-in-chief

After taking the customary oath or making affirmation, a witness gives evidence, assisted by the lawyer representing the side for which they are appearing. This is called examination-in-chief.

Cross-examination

The lawyer appearing for the other side (the defence) then has the right to ask the witness questions in an attempt to negate or diminish that evidence by, for example, casting doubt on the memory, accuracy or hearing of the witness. This is called cross-examination. After a cross examination the lawyer representing the witness's side can re-examine in order to explain or remove ambiguity in any answer given during cross-examination.

Leading questions

A question so framed as to suggest to a witness what answer is required is not usually permitted. For example: 'Did you see A take some money from the coats in the cloakroom?' would be disallowed. The proper question would be: 'What did you see A do?'

Perjury

This is a serious offence committed by a witness who, while under oath or affirmation, gives evidence that is known to be false or not known to be true and which is material to the proceedings.

Giving evidence

Before giving evidence in court a witness will usually be seen by the police officer involved in the case. At this point the witness will be able to refresh their memory by reading any statement made to the police. The police officer will also be available to discuss court procedure with the witness. Also, most crown courts now have witness liaison officers who are there to assist witnesses with any matters of concern.

When the case in which the witness is to give evidence is about to be heard, any witness inside the courtroom will be asked to leave and wait to be called by the usher or some other court official.

Security officers should be dressed in their best uniform and of a clean and neat appearance. Once in the witness box they should stand smartly, not put hands in their pockets, and not lean against the side of the box.

Witnesses will be called upon in court to give their full name, address and occupation, and to take the oath or affirmation. The court usher will lead the witness through this procedure.

When giving evidence, the witness will be able to make reference to notes made at the time, such as those contained in a notebook. However, to make such a reference the witness must ask the court's permission. Referral to notes must not be made unless it is absolutely necessary. Any exhibits the witness is required to produce will be handed to the witness once they are in the witness box.

A High Court judge should be addressed as 'My Lord', a crown court judge as 'Your Honour', a magistrate as 'Your Worship' and a coroner as 'Sir'. Questions from any court official should be answered without equivocation and with complete fairness. The witness must not argue with the questioner and must ask for a question to be repeated if it is not understood. If a mistake is made in giving evidence, it should be admitted at once. The composure of the witness should not be compromised by histrionics from defending lawyers – often a tactical measure used to discredit evidence that cannot otherwise be disproved.

At the end of giving evidence the witness must not leave the witness box until told to do so by the court. If the case is one that may be transferred to the High Court, the witness will be required to sign a deposition – a written record of what has been said. The witness may be called to repeat it in the High Court.

PROSECUTION OF OFFENDERS

All prosecutions in England and Wales are conducted by the Crown Prosecution Service (CPS), not the police. The Crown Prosecutor is empowered to decide whether to instigate proceedings, take no action, discontinue proceedings or take over proceedings that have already commenced. The Crown Prosecutor may choose charges to be preferred and shall advise whether a matter should be tried summarily or on indictment.

JURISDICTION OF COURTS

A youth court deals with most summary and indictable offences committed by children and persons aged 17 and under. A child under ten in England and Wales (under eight in Scotland) cannot be prosecuted because a child of that age is not deemed responsible in law. Proceedings in youth courts are less formal than in other courts and access by the general public is restricted. Magistrates are drawn from a panel of those specially qualified to deal with young people. They can impose a wide range of penalties, but not commit to prison.

A magistrates' court hears all the less serious offences and commits the more serious ones to crown courts. These hearings are presided over by justices of the peace or a stipendiary magistrate.

The crown court deals with all serious offences involving trial by jury. Appeals from its verdicts or sentences are referred to the Court of Criminal Appeal, which in turn may permit a further appeal on a matter deemed of significant importance (almost always one of legal interpretation) to the House of Lords, which is the highest court for England and Wales.

WITNESS STATEMENTS

Where evidence is not contentious, it may be presented to a court in the form of a written and signed statement from the witness who is not required to attend and give evidence personally. Conditions are attached to this, and an original statement that is likely to be redrafted should be checked by the witness for accuracy before signature. Statutory declarations are acceptable in lieu of personal evidence on matters of a purely routine nature, such as the dispatch, receipt or non-receipt of goods in transit.

A witness summons can be served on persons unwilling to attend court to give evidence. Certain categories of witness can claim 'privilege' and be exempted, such as lawyers in respect of their clients' affairs and priests in respect of confessions.

WITNESS SUPPORT AND PROTECTION

It is a criminal offence to intimidate a witness or anyone helping the police in an investigation. Anyone harassed or threatened in any way before, during or after a trial should tell the police immediately. Now that the CPS and the police work more closely together on witness care, they can protect the identity of a witness during the investigation prior to a trial and during the early stages of the prosecution process. In exceptional cases, the identity of a witness can be protected throughout the trial itself. Working in partnership with local authorities, in the more extreme circumstances the police may be able to relocate victims and witnesses.

Most courts have staff available to give support to witnesses. They will explain the procedures to the witness and may even let them have a look round a courtroom so as to familiarise themselves with the surroundings. Indeed, every care is taken to ensure that witnesses have as comfortable an experience as possible.

16 Industrial or Trade Disputes

The police are responsible for preserving the peace and upholding the law against pickets outside the perimeter of premises where there is a dispute. However, security staff must be aware of any management instructions about the access of strikers or their union representatives to the premises.

It is probable that during a dispute security staff will be engaged principally in the protection of the premises and the prevention of any undue disruption within the premises by those involved in the dispute.

LEGISLATION

The principal statutes relating to industrial or trade dispute law are:

- the Trade Unions and Labour Relations (Consolidation) Act 1992;
- the Trade Union Reforms and Employment Rights Act 1993.

However, these statutes conflict to some degree with Article 11 of the Human Rights Act 1998, which states that everyone has the right to freedom of peaceful assembly and to freedom of association with others, including the right to form and to join trade unions for the protection of his or her interests. The key word here is 'peaceful'.

DEFINITION OF AN INDUSTRIAL OR TRADE DISPUTE

The reasons for an industrial or trade dispute are many, and they are briefly described in this text. An industrial or trade dispute is defined as a dispute between workers and their employer that relates wholly or mainly to:

- terms and conditions of employment;
- the physical health and safety conditions in which workers have to work;
- membership or non-membership of trade unions;

- the type of work the worker is expected to do;
- matters of discipline;
- a breakdown in the machinery for negotiation or consultation about the rights of workers.

PEACEFUL PICKETING

Trade union law does allow for peaceful picketing and makes it lawful for a person in the furtherance of a trade dispute to attend at or near his place of work, or if he is an official of a trade union, at or near to the place of work of a person who he is accompanying and representing, for the purpose of peacefully obtaining or communicating information or peacefully persuading any person to work or not to work.

Where an employee works at more than one of the company's premises, that employee may peacefully picket at any of those premises.

INTIMIDATION AND ANNOYANCE TO THOSE INVOLVED IN A TRADE DISPUTE

The legislation makes it an offence for a person to compel a person to stop doing or to do something that the person has a legal right to do or abstain from doing, wrongfully and without legal authority, for example in the following circumstances:

- Using violence or intimidating the person or his family or damaging his property, including frightening people by exhibiting force or using threats of violence.
- Persistently following the person from place to place.
- Hiding property used or owned by that person, such as tools and clothes.
- Watching the house or place where the person resides, works or where business is carried out. Peaceful picketing legislation does not permit the watching of a private residence in any circumstances.
- Following that person with two or more other persons in a disorderly manner along any street or road.

These offences could be committed against a security officer whose role is to prevent damage, theft and unlawful intrusion at the place involved in the dispute. In an increasingly volatile dispute, security officers should be prepared for threats and intimidation from those hostile to their employer.

DUTIES OF SECURITY STAFF

The main duty of security personnel in trade and industrial disputes is to remain professional and impartial. Other duties may include:

- Being familiar with company rules and procedures, particularly those laid down for dealing with trade and industrial disputes.

- Ensuring the privacy of the premises and the business by excluding intruders, potential thieves, unwanted callers and trespassers.

- Preventing theft from and damage to the premises.

- Recording and controlling the movement of vehicles that have a legitimate right to be on the site.

- Continuing normal duties, but not undertaking additional duties except as part of a contract with the employer or to save life.

- Remembering that goodwill is an important factor in relationships with others, and to be helpful and consistent in dealings with all parties concerned in the dispute.

- Not becoming involved in acrimonious exchanges with those in dispute.

- Not permitting those in dispute to enter the premises without management authority.

- Not carrying out overt actions that could be construed as collecting information for victimisation purposes.

- Not acting as if security has the authority or powers of a police officer.

- Remaining courteous, even under the most extreme provocation.

- Remaining impartial and unbiased at all times.

Although there appears to have been fewer industrial disputes in recent times, the security professional needs to be aware of the complex issues that surround such disputes. When agreeing the role with employers, contract negotiators need to be clear about the perceived responsibility that the organisation's management has for security personnel during such disputes.

17 Health and Safety and Accident Prevention

Accidents at work can lead to substantial personal suffering and loss of productivity and profitability to the employer. Accidents must therefore be a matter of general concern to security personnel, who should exercise a helpful and observant role in the interests of both fellow employees and the employer. The Health and Safety at Work Act 1974 imposes obligations on employers and individuals to minimise risks and provides for penalties where obligations are not met. Knowledge of the Act's key provisions is therefore necessary.

HEALTH AND SAFETY AT WORK ACT 1974

The objectives of the Act are to secure the health, safety and welfare of persons at work, to protect the public against risks arising out of business activity, to control the obtaining, keeping and use of explosives and other dangerous materials, and to control the discharge of noxious fumes.

To achieve these objectives, specific duties are laid upon employers and employees and there are penal consequences for non-compliance with the legislation.

Section 2 of the Act states that, so far as is reasonably practicable, the employer must ensure the health, safety and welfare at work of all his employees. The employer must:

- provide and maintain risk-free plant and procedures;
- ensure safe use, handling, storage and transport of materials;
- provide information, instruction, training and supervision;
- provide and maintain a safe and healthy place of work with adequate means of access and egress;
- provide a satisfactory working environment, adequate in facilities and welfare arrangements.

The Management of Health and Safety at Work Regulations 1992 places two requirements on employers:

1. To make a suitable and sufficient assessment of the risks to the health and safety of their employees to which they are exposed while they are at work.

2. To make an assessment of the risks to the health and safety of persons not in their employment arising out of or in connection with the conduct by themselves or their employees.

Under Section 3 of the Act, employers must also ensure, as far as is reasonably practicable, the health, safety and welfare of people who are not in their employ, but who are on the premises. This covers contractors, including contracted security staff and visitors.

Under Section 7 of the Act employees too have a duty of care to themselves and for others who may be affected by their acts or omissions, and also a duty to cooperate with the employer in complying with the legislation. Security may have to report misbehaviour for disciplinary purposes: Section 8 of the 1974 Act says, 'No person shall intentionally or recklessly interfere with or misuse anything provided in the interests of health and safety'.

Enforcement

A Health and Safety Executive inspector, who must carry proof of identity and authority for production on request, has the power to (in brief):

- enter any premises at any reasonable time to carry out their responsibilities;

- ask assistance from the police if necessary;

- take along expert assistance and equipment;

- investigate any activity while inside the premises;

- order premises and plant to be left undisturbed as long as is reasonably required so that the job can be carried out there;

- take samples of articles and substances or carry out atmospheric tests;

- have articles and substances dismantled or tested or take temporary possession of them;

- require answers to questions and to take statements;

- ask for such assistance and facilities as a person has the right to give;

- demand production of statutory books and documents required to be seen in connection with the visit.

Penalties

Fines on indictment, coupled with imprisonment, can be imposed for a wide variety of offences. The main penal section (Section 33 of the 1974 Act) covers failure to discharge duties, misuse or interference by employees, contravention of requirements, failure to comply with notices, falsification of records and so on. There are especially heavy penalties for intentional obstruction of any person exercising powers under the Act, for preventing a person being seen by an inspector, for not answering an inspector's questions, for intentionally obstructing an inspector or for pretending to be an inspector.

This is wide-reaching legislation with serious implications, and security should take due note.

PATROLLING SECURITY OFFICERS' DUTIES

The security officer must not approach a worker engaged in what is thought to be a dangerous practice unless danger is imminent. The worker's supervisor must be informed of the dangerous practice. Where anything is seen to be a safety issue, the company safety officer should be informed and an entry must be made in the occurrence book so that other colleagues are aware that the matter is receiving attention.

The security officer must not usurp the company safety officer's responsibilities. Points security officers should look out for are as follows:

- patches of oil or grease that constitute a danger on roads and footways;
- protruding slabs or cavities in footways, broken tiles, holes in tiled floors and loose floorboards;
- defective lighting over staircases or at any place where people may have access after dark;
- defective stair-treads or badly worn or broken stair edges;
- broken or defective handrails;
- damaged ladders;
- obstruction of gangways, fire points and exits;
- dangerous stacking of materials;
- leaking valves and joints;

- repeated dangerous parking of vehicles;

- reckless or dangerous driving of vehicles;

- unauthorised riding on fork-lift trucks;

- failure to use protective equipment in dangerous working areas where specific requirements are laid down in company regulations;

- unattended loads left suspended on overhead cranes;

- horse-play by employees anywhere in the premises, but especially near machinery;

- deliberate interference with anything provided for first aid, welfare or fire safety purposes;

- unauthorised personnel interfering with electric services and switch-gear;

- indications of dangerous fumes or gases;

- spilling of scalding, corrosive or poisonous liquids;

- excessive accumulations of refuse in working areas or passages;

- faulty dust-extraction or ventilating equipment;

- dangerous practices by contractors during alterations or other work.

These issues are primarily associated with industrial premises, but the same principles of watchful care should be observed by security officers in whatever environment they are employed.

ACTION AT ACCIDENTS

- Render first aid and ensure there is immediate expert attention and removal to hospital if required.

- Obtain details of all persons who have witnessed or have knowledge of the accident and get a brief account from them of how it occurred.

- Obtain full details of the injured person, their job, their works department and the name of their supervisor.

- Obtain from the injured person, if possible, a version of what happened.

- Leave all the details of the accident in a report for the company safety officer.

- Indicate the nature of the injuries and where the casualty has been taken if removed to a hospital or sent home.

- If the accident is a serious one, ensure the safety officer and management are informed as soon as possible and that nothing that has any bearing on the accident is moved from the scene. In the case of a fatal or possible fatal accident, consider roping off the area until the Health and Safety Executive inspector and the police have arrived and inspected and photographed the scene.

- If an injured person is to be detained beyond the time he or she would normally return home, ensure that arrangements are made to warn relatives of the whereabouts of the casualty.

- Be available to the police and the Health and Safety Executive inspector, and give them your full assistance wherever possible.

18 Fire Precautions

The prevention, detection and extinguishing of fire are a fundamental part of security duties. Apart from knowing how to recognise hazards, handle equipment and patrol to the best advantage, the security officer must have some knowledge of the legal requirements to counter fire and of the causes of outbreaks.

REGULATORY REFORM (FIRE SAFETY) ORDER 2005

The Regulatory Reform (Fire Safety) Order (referred to in the remainder of this chapter as 'the Fire Safety Order') became law on 1 October 2006. This new legislation repeals the Fire Precautions Act 1971 and is designed to provide greater emphasis on fire prevention in all non-domestic premises, including in the voluntary sector and for self-employed people with premises separate from their homes. The Fire Safety Order covers 'general fire precautions' and other fire safety duties that are needed to protect 'relevant people' against fire in and around most non-domestic premises.

The most important objective of this and other associated legislation is the protection of life and, to that end, the Fire Safety Order's various provisions are designed to reduce the threat that fire poses to human life. The Fire Safety Order, which abolishes the need for fire certificates, requires fire precautions to be put in place where necessary and to the extent that it is reasonable and practicable in the circumstances, and the responsibility for complying with the Fire Safety Order rests with the 'responsible person'.

The following represents a summary of the main contents of the Fire Safety Order that are likely to affect the work of security officers.

The 'responsible person' and their fire safety duties (sections 3 and 4)

The 'responsible person' is the person who owns or controls the business or premises, and where two or more persons share these responsibilities (such as landlord and tenant) they are obliged to cooperate. This person is responsible for the safety of employees and other relevant persons by properly managing 'general fire precautions', such as:

- risk assessment
- fire drills and evacuation
- means of escape
- signs and notices
- fire alarms and emergency lighting
- fire doors and compartments
- staff training.

Premises

The Fire Safety Order defines 'premises' as including any place, and in particular, any workplace, any vehicle, vessel, aircraft or hovercraft and any tent or movable structure.

General fire precautions (section 8)

The 'responsible person' must take such general fire precautions as will ensure, so far as is reasonably practicable, the safety of any employees, and in relation to relevant persons who are not employees, take such general fire precautions as may reasonably be required in the circumstances of the case to ensure the premises are safe. People who are not employees of the 'responsible person' may be visitors, customers or contracted service providers, including contract security staff.

Risk assessment (section 9)

The 'responsible person' must make suitable and sufficient assessment of the risks to which persons are exposed for the purpose of identifying the general fire precautions needed in order to comply with the requirements and prohibitions imposed by the Fire Safety Order. This includes where a substance is or is liable to be present in or on the premises. Matters to be considered include the types and substances used, their quantities, the risk of any effects resulting from the combination of two or more substances, the likelihood of ignition sources, the likelihood of explosion and the scale of the anticipated effects.

The risk assessment must be reviewed and updated regularly by the responsible person, particularly where the assessment is deemed to be no longer valid or where there has been a significant change in matters to which the assessment relates.

Where the responsible person employs five or more employees, as soon as practicable after the risk assessment has been made or reviewed, significant findings must be recorded, including the measures that have been or will be taken pursuant to the Fire Safety Order, and identifying any individuals or groups who may be especially at risk. Any new work activity involving dangerous substances may not commence unless the risk assessment has been made and the measures required under the Fire Safety Order have been implemented.

Fire safety arrangements (section 11)

The 'responsible person' must make and give effect to such arrangements as are appropriate, having regard to the size and nature of their undertaking and its activities, for the effective planning, organisation, control, monitoring and review of the protective and preventive measures. These arrangements must be made where five or more people are employed, where there is any other licence in force relating to the premises (such as a justices' on licence) or any alterations notice that has been issued requiring a record to be made of the fire safety arrangements that are in place relating to the premises.

Dangerous substances (section 12)

Where dangerous substances are present on the premises, the 'responsible person' must ensure that the risk to relevant persons in relation to the presence of such substances is either eliminated or reduced so far as is reasonably practicable. The Fire Safety Order goes on to say that, so far as is reasonably practicable, the 'responsible person' should replace the dangerous substance or the use of it with a substance or process that eliminates or reduces the risk.

Fire-fighting and detection (section 13)

For the detection and fighting of fire, the 'responsible person' must ensure that:

- the premises are equipped with appropriate fire-fighting equipment and with fire detectors and alarms; and
- any non-automatic fire-fighting equipment is easily accessible, simple to use and indicated by signs.

The appropriateness of non-automatic fire-fighting equipment is influenced by the physical and chemical properties of substances likely to be on the premises and the maximum number of people who are likely to be there at any one time.

The 'responsible person' must also:

- Nominate competent persons to implement the measures and to ensure that these people are suitably trained in the use of the equipment and that the equipment provided for their use is suitable in the circumstances, taking into account the activities carried out on the premises, the specific hazards and the size of the premises.
- Arrange any necessary contacts with external emergency services in relation to fire-fighting, rescue work, first aid and emergency medical care.

Emergency routes and exits (section 14)

The 'responsible person' must ensure that emergency routes and exits are clear from obstruction at all times. This is an essential duty of the security officer, who must bring to the attention of management any location that compromises the legal duty of the responsible person. Other duties include:

- Ensuring that emergency exit routes lead as directly as possible to a place of safety and that the premises can be evacuated quickly and safely.
- Ensuring that the number of emergency exit routes and doors are adequate and commensurate with the size of the premises,

the maximum number of occupants who are likely to be on the premises at any one time and the fire-fighting equipment available.

- Ensuring that the emergency exit doors open in the direction of escape, are not locked and can be opened easily by any person who may need to exit in an emergency.

- Ensuring that sliding or revolving doors are not used for evacuating the premises.

- Ensuring that routes and exits are appropriately signed and that exit routes are adequately lit.

Procedures for serious and imminent danger and for danger areas (section 15)

The 'responsible person' must establish procedures and safety drills to be followed in the event of serious or imminent danger, and must nominate competent people to carry out evacuation procedures. Some organisations label these people as 'Fire Marshals'. Section 15 also mandates that no person, unless they have been given adequate safety instruction, should have access to any area where it is necessary to restrict access on safety grounds.

Where reasonably practicable, persons exposed to serious and imminent danger must be informed of the nature of the hazard and the steps taken to protect them from it. The section also makes provision for work to be halted immediately where there is imminent danger, for workers to be evacuated to a place of safety and preventing people returning to work where there is still serious or imminent danger.

Provision of information to employees (section 19)

The 'responsible person' must provide employees with information on:

- risks identified by risk assessment;

- protective and preventive measures;

- procedures and drills necessary in the event of serious and imminent danger;

- the identity of people who have been trained in evacuation procedures.

The responsible person must also notify employees of the presence of dangerous substances in the workplace and the risks they present.

Security professionals contracted in to premises must have a grasp of the organisation's procedures and should be aware of any dangerous substances that are on the premises. In an ideal world, this information should be made available to the contractor during contract negotiations. If it is not, the negotiator should ask for it when seeking information about the organisation's profile.

General duties of employees (section 23)

The general duties of employees differ little from those required under the Health and Safety at Work Act 1974 (see Chapter 17). In brief, every employee must:

- Take reasonable care for their own safety and the safety of others who may be affected by their acts or omissions.

- Cooperate with the employer as regards any duty requirements imposed by the Fire Safety Order on the employer.

- Inform the employer and safety representative of any work situation that represents a serious and immediate danger to safety and of any matter that the employee would reasonably consider to represent a shortcoming in the employer's safety protection arrangements.

Security professionals must have knowledge of the organisation's business so that they can identify situations where there may be a shortcoming in the employer's safety protection arrangements.

Inspection of premises (section 27)

An authorised fire authority inspector may enter (at any reasonable time) all parts of premises to which the Fire Safety Order applies in order to:

- Inspect the whole or part of the premises.

- Make such enquiries as are necessary to find out if the provisions of the Fire Safety Order are being complied with.

- Identify the responsible person in relation to the premises.

- Require the production of extracts from fire safety records for the purposes of examination, inspection or to take copies.

- Require the responsible person to afford such facilities and
  assistance to allow the inspector to exercise any powers conferred
  by the Fire Safety Order.

- Take samples of any articles or substances found on the premises
  to test their fire resistance or flammability, and in the case of any
  article or substance likely to cause danger to the safety of people,
  cause it to be dismantled or subjected to any process or test.

Enforcement notices (section 30)

If the enforcing authority believes that the 'responsible person' has failed to
comply with the provisions of the Fire Safety Order, the authority may serve
an enforcement notice on that person. The enforcement notice must:

- State that the enforcing authority is of the opinion that the
  responsible person has failed to comply with the provisions of the
  Fire Safety Order.

- Specify the provisions that have not been complied with.

- Require that person to take steps to remedy the failure within 28
  days from the date of service of the notice.

Prohibition notices (section 31)

A prohibition notice may be issued to premises where the enforcing
agency is of the opinion that the risk to people (including fire risk) is so
serious that the use of the premises ought to be restricted or prohibited.
The notice must:

- State that the enforcing authority is of the opinion that the risk
  is so serious that the use of the premises must be prohibited or
  restricted.

- Specify the matters that in their opinion give rise to the risk.

- Direct that the use to which the notice relates is prohibited or
  restricted to such an extent as may be specified in the notice until
  the matters have been remedied.

The prohibition notice may include directions as to the measures that
will have to be taken to remedy the matters specified in the notice. The
prohibition takes effect as soon as the notice is served.

CLASSIFICATIONS OF FIRE

There are five main types of fire risk, each requiring the use of specific extinguishing agents. British Standard 4547 classifies these risks according to the materials involved and the extinguishing media needed to extinguish the fire. The classes of fire are:

- *Class A*. Fires involving solid, normally carbonaceous materials, which form glowing embers such as paper, wood and their derivatives.

- *Class B*. Fires involving liquids or liquefiable solids, such as oils, fats, petroleum jellies, petrol, paraffin and so on.

- *Class C*. Fires involving gases or liquefied gases in jet or spray form, such as propane, butane, methane and so on.

- *Class D*. Fires involving metals.

- *Class E*. Fires involving electrical appliances.

CODES AND STANDARDS

To determine what type of fire extinguishing equipment is appropriate for individual circumstances information is issued in the form of codes and guides.

Sale and servicing of fire-fighting equipment

Fire services do not sell or service fire-fighting equipment, nor do they recommend particular brands or makes. However, they do recommend that service contracts should only be entered into with companies that are members of a reputable trade organisation such as FETA (the Fire Extinguishing Trades Association).

Under current standards, all extinguishers are predominantly red in colour. The former practice of colouring the extinguisher body to indicate its contents – for example, blue for dry powder type – no longer applies. Instead, manufacturer's now make extinguishers with up to 5 per cent of the red body coloured differently to indicate contents. The differently coloured area will be on the front of the extinguisher, next to, or on the instruction label. The colours are:

- red – water
- cream – foam
- blue – dry powder
- black – carbon dioxide CO_2.

These rules only apply to new extinguishers. Existing extinguishers can continue to be used until the end of their useful lives (see Table 18.1 later in this chapter).

Training

Whether or not staff should tackle an outbreak of fire as part of their fire procedure is a matter of company policy. This should be made clear on any fire procedure notices. If staff are instructed to fight fire, they must be competent to use the equipment provided. Although first aid fire-fighting equipment is usually marked with instructions for use, it is wise to provide competent instruction. Instruction can be provided by:

- the company that services the fire-fighting equipment;
- the local county or metropolitan fire service;
- other commercial training providers.

ESSENTIAL PRECAUTIONS

Some of the essential precautions when fighting fire are listed below:

- Do not overestimate your single-handed capabilities at fire extinction. Call the fire service immediately on discovery of a fire. Arrange for liaison with the fire service officer in charge, guide them to the scene, and provide them with any information they might need to successfully and safely extinguish the fire, such as the presence of any dangerous installation, explosives, highly inflammable substances, corrosive substances and so on.
- Memorise where fire-fighting appliances are sited and know which are dangerous to use on particular types of fire.
- Never attack a fire from a point where the fire is between you and a means of escape.
- If it is necessary to enter a smoke-filled room – for example to save life – do so at floor level and with assistance to hand in case you are overcome.

MAIN CAUSES OF FIRE

Electrical faults

These may be due to:

- overloading of circuits beyond their capacity;
- equipment overloaded mechanically or overheated because of inadequate ventilation;
- short circuits caused by damage to insulation;
- careless or inefficient maintenance.

Heating appliances

Most types of heating appliances are harmless if correctly installed, sited and maintained, but portable heaters, gas and electric fires, stoves, open fires, steam and hot water pipes are dangerous if:

- they are placed on an unstable or flammable base;
- they are placed in proximity to flammable material;
- they generate sparks or are apt to flare up in draughts.

Process dangers

These are usually accidental or due to careless operating. For example:

- accidental ignition of flammable liquids or gases, including fires resulting from spilling liquids;
- accidental overheating of substances undergoing processing;
- flame failure in heating equipment causing explosion and fire;
- frictional heat and spark emission;
- failure of ventilation or cooling devices;
- chemical reactions getting out of hand.

Static electricity

This is dangerous where solvent vapours or explosives are in use. All machinery should be bonded to the earth and the humidity increased.

Flammable dusts

Finely divided and in adequate concentration, certain metallic or carbonaceous dusts can form an explosive cloud. Excess dust in roof voids can smoulder unobserved and then break into a sudden flare-up over an entire area.

Spontaneous combustion

A variety of substances, by decomposition or chemical reaction, progressively heat up to ignition point without the assistance of any outside agency other than oxygen. Oily rags, sacks and oil seeds are examples of substances that should be cleared regularly or kept in fireproof containers.

Carelessness

Rank carelessness is probably the main cause of fire, and can result from the following:

- thoughtless disposal of cigarette ends in waste paper baskets;
- smoking in prohibited areas;
- leaving blow lamps of welding equipment burning;
- failing to check the scene where heat and burning have been applied before leaving it, such as where welding repair work has been carried out in roof structures;
- general disregard of works regulations designed to reduce fire risk.

FIRE PATROLLING

When on fire patrol, the security officer should inspect all parts of the premises as soon as possible after they have been vacated, and systematically at intervals thereafter, paying special attention to known danger points. Inspection should not be confined to floor level. Many fires start in roofs that house electric cabling and ventilation conduits and are first seen when they break through ceilings. The officer must not overlook the exterior of the premises and must pay attention to places where timber and flammable materials are stacked outside or are exposed to vandalism. The officer must check that such items are stacked away from perimeter fencing. Other special points to be borne in mind when patrolling are:

- Switch off any electric fires and heaters left on unless it is essential that they be on.

- Switch off gas and electric cooking facilities and investigate any smells of gas or burning.

- Switch off plant accidentally left running and not in use. Check any plant that is cooling down.

- Extinguish naked flames and check that soldering irons and similar items are disconnected.

- Clear overalls and other flammable materials from heaters and replace any missing fireguards.

- Move away from sources of heat anything that is apt to burn, and check combustible materials left in boiler houses.

- Close internal doors so as to inhibit the spread of fire.

- Stop and report any leakage of oil or flammable liquids immediately.

- In offices, glance at waste paper bins to check that no smouldering fire has been caused by discarded cigarettes.

- Check that all fire-fighting equipment is present, serviceable and unobstructed, that access to hydrants is clear, fire alarm points are intact and sprinkler heads are not obstructed by stacked goods.

- Ensure that avenues of access for the fire service are unimpeded.

- Where automatic processes involving heat are functioning, visit them regularly to make sure all are in order.

- Visit and check areas where welding or other hot working has taken place, especially roofs where there may be dust-shrouded smouldering.

- If your sense of smell suggests something may be wrong, investigate.

The security officer should note and report on any such instances to prevent their repetition.

INDICATIONS OF ARSON

These include:

- simultaneous outbreak of fire in separate places;
- several isolated and unconnected points of ignition;
- the presence of flammable materials foreign to the area concerned;
- the presence of burnt-out petrol cans or similar containers;
- the smell or indication of flammable liquids that should not be there;
- indications that the premises have been broken into;
- prior threats, previous occurrences and an unlikely time of outbreak.

If there is any doubt in the security officer's mind as to the cause of a fire, the police must be informed and the officer should take care to ensure that nothing is moved from the scene of the incident.

FIRE-FIGHTING AND EXTINGUISHANTS

A detailed list of extinguishants is set out in Table 18.1.

Fire blankets

Fire blankets are classified in BS 7944 and are described as follows:

- *Light duty*. These are suitable for dealing with small fires in containers of cooking fat, oils or fires in clothing.
- *Heavy duty*. These are for industrial use where there is a need for the blanket to resist penetration by molten materials.

Table 18.1   Fire-fighting and extinguishants

Type/Colour	How it works	Danger	How to use
Standard dry powder or multi-purpose dry powder (blue)	**Standard dry powder** knocks down flames. Best used for liquids such as grease, fats, oil, paint, petrol but *not* for chip or fat pan fires **Multi-purpose dry powder** knocks down flames, and on burning solids it melts to form a skin that smothers the fire. Provides some cooling. It is best for wood, cloth, paper, plastics, any solids and liquids such as grease, fats, oils, paint, petrol and so on, but *not* chip or pan fires	This type of extinguisher does not cool the fire very well. Care must be taken to ensure that the fire does not reignite. Although safe to use on electrical equipment, it does not readily penetrate spaces inside equipment. To stop reignition the power supply should be isolated. Smouldering material in a deep-seated fire can cause reignition.	Point the jet discharge horn at the base of the flames and, with a rapid sweeping motion, drive the fire towards the far edge until the flames are out. If the extinguisher has a shut-off control, wait until the air clears and, where the flames are visible, attack the fire again
Water (red)	**Water** works mainly by cooling burning material. It is best used on wood, cloth, paper, plastics, coal and so on and generally all fires involving solids	Do *not* use on burning fat or oil or on electrical appliances	Point the jet at the base of the flame and keep it moving across the area of the fire. Ensure that all areas of the fire are out

Type/Colour	How it works	Danger	How to use
AFFF (aqueous film-forming) multi-purpose (yellow)	**AFFF** forms an extinguishing film on the surface of burning liquids. It has a cooling action with a wider extinguishing application than water on solids and combustible materials. It is best used on wood, cloth, paper, plastic and so on, and liquids such as grease, fats, oils, paint and so on, but *not* chip or pan fires	Not recommended for home use	Point the jet at the base of the flame and keep it moving across the area of the fire. Ensure that all areas of the fire are out. If liquids are involved, do not aim the jet straight into the liquid. If the liquid is in a container, point the jet at the inside edge of the container or nearby surface above the burning liquid. Allow foam to build up and flow across the liquid
Carbon dioxide CO_2 (black)	**CO_2** vaporising liquid gas smothers the flames by displacing oxygen in the air. It is best for liquids such as grease, fats, oil, paint, petrol and so on, but *not* chip and pan fires. It is clean and effective and safe on electrical fires	Does not cool fire very well and has to be watched for reignition. It can be harmful in confined spaces as it displaces oxygen. The area should be ventilated as soon as the fire is extinguished	The discharge horn should be directed at the base of the flames and the jet kept moving across the areas of the fire

Type/Colour	How it works	Danger	How to use
Foam (cream)	***Foam*** forms a blanket over the surface of the burning liquid and smothers the fire. It is best for a limited number of liquid fires, so the manufacturer's instructions should be checked for suitability on fires involving liquids	Not recommended for home use	Point the jet at the base of the flames and keep it moving across the area of the fire. Ensure that all areas of the fire are out. For fires involving liquids, do not aim the jet straight into the liquid. If the liquid is in a container, point the jet at the inside edge of the container or nearby surface above the burning liquid. Allow foam to build up and flow across the liquid
Vaporising liquid (including halon) (green)	***Vaporising liquid*** is a liquid gas that gives a rapid knock-down by chemically inhibiting combustion. It is best for liquids such as grease, fats, oil, paint, petrol and so on but *not* chip and pan fires	Does not cool fire very well. Care should be taken to ensure no reignition. Fumes from the extinguisher can be harmful in confined spaces, particularly if used on hot metal. The area should be well ventilated as soon as the fire has been extinguished	The vaporising liquid is expelled in a jet which should *not* be aimed into burning liquids as this increases the risk of spreading the fire. The discharge nozzle should be aimed at the flames and kept moving across the fire. (Owing to the ozone-depleting potential of halon, its future use and availability will be restricted)

Essential precautions when using extinguishers

Key points are as follows:

- do not use water jets on electrical fires;
- do not use water jets on oil fires;
- protect all appliances containing water from frost;
- do not return a used extinguisher to its station without ensuring that it will be immediately replaced;
- ensure that all extinguishers are tested and serviced regularly and that a tag is attached showing the date of the last test.

POINTS TO BE INCLUDED IN A FIRE REPORT

- Time, date, area of outbreak and details of the person finding the fire.
- Time and date when last seen in order and by whom.
- Times of notification, arrival and departure of the fire service attending.
- Name of the officer in charge of the fire service attending and the means of maintaining contact.
- The precise location of the outbreak of fire.
- A general description of the fire, including details of the structures or equipment damaged and any services affected such as gas, electricity and water services.
- The cause of the fire if this information is available from the fire officer in charge.
- The senior personnel notified of the outbreak and the times of the notification. The time of notifying a fire assessor should also be noted if there is an instruction that such a person should be informed.

A note of minor fires should be made in the occurrence book in case smouldering material has not been noticed.

19 Dealing with Emergencies

Section 1 of the Civil Contingencies Act 2004 defines an emergency as being:

An event or situation which threatens serious damage to human welfare; an event or situation which threatens serious damage to the environment; or war, or terrorism, which threatens serious damage to security.

A major disaster may be defined as:

A serious disruption to life, arising with little or no warning, causing or threatening death or serious injury to such number of persons, in excess of those which can be dealt with by public services operating under normal conditions at the time, that calls for special mobilisation and organisation of those services.

EMERGENCY PROCEDURES

The Civil Contingencies Act 2004 is designed to provide a single framework based on local arrangements to deal with emergencies and disasters. It focuses on local arrangements for civil protection, establishing a statutory framework of roles and responsibilities for local councils and emergency services. However, plans need to be made where there is a threat of major disaster or emergency to individual organisations, and this is where security staff will have a key role to play.

THE ROLE OF SECURITY

In the event of a major incident, the role of security professionals will be significant and critical to the effective management of the incident. Their functions will include:

- being vigilant to the threat of theft or looting;
- establishing an inner and outer cordon;

- responsibility for access control (ensuring access for the emergency services, restricting access to individuals and so on);

- controlling and directing traffic;

- directing the media to the public relations officer, who should be available outside the outer cordon;

- checking and securing buildings not affected by the emergency;

- bringing to the attention of the police any evidence that the incident was caused maliciously;

- assisting the emergency services when requested.

TERRORISM

Dictionary definitions of terrorism centre on the creation of fear or intimidation in pursuit of an aim. While the United Kingdom has faced a variety of terrorist threats in the past, a unique combination of factors – principally the global reach, capability, resilience, sophistication, ambition and lack of restraint of Al Qaeda and associated groups from around the world – place the current threat on a scale not previously encountered.

The security officer can play a key role in supporting the police. By remaining vigilant and being security-minded, the security officer can help protect business, commerce and individuals against crime and make the work of terrorists more difficult.

Suicide bombers

The suicide attacks in New York and London make clear that this tactic has now become a threat to parts of the world previously untouched by suicide terrorism.

Suicide bombers may use a lorry, plane or other kind of vehicle as a bomb, either carrying explosives or, in the case of planes, using the fuel aboard as a makeshift explosive. Also, they may conceal explosives on their person. Both kinds of attack are generally perpetrated without warning. The most likely targets are symbolic locations, key installations, VIPs or mass-casualty 'soft' targets.

When considering protective measures against suicide bombers:

- Deny access to anyone or anything that has not been thoroughly searched. Ensure that no one visits a protected area without your being sure of his or her identity or without proper authority.

- Establish your search area at a distance from the protected site, setting up regular patrols and briefing staff to look out for anyone behaving suspiciously. Many bomb attacks are preceded by reconnaissance or trial runs, so ensure that any incidents are reported to the police.

- Effective CCTV systems can help prevent or even deter hostile reconnaissance, and can provide crucial evidence in court.

- There is no definitive physical profile for a suicide bomber, so remain vigilant and report anyone suspicious to the police.

CHEMICAL, BIOLOGICAL AND RADIOLOGICAL ATTACKS

Since the early 1990s, concern that terrorists might use chemical, biological and radiological (CBR) materials as weapons has steadily increased. CBR is a general term that covers three distinct groups of hazards:

1. *Chemical.* Poisoning or injury caused by chemical substances, including former military chemical warfare agents or legitimate but harmful household or industrial chemicals.

2. *Biological.* Illnesses caused by the deliberate release of dangerous bacteria, viruses or fungi, or biological toxins such as Ricin, a natural toxin occurring in plants.

3. *Radiological (radioactive).* Illness caused by exposure to harmful radioactive materials contaminating the environment.

Much of the CBR-related activity seen to date has either been criminal, or has involved hoaxes and false alarms. There have so far only been a few examples of terrorists using CBR materials. The most notable were the 1995 sarin gas attack that killed 12 people on the Tokyo subway, and the 2001 anthrax letters in the United States, which killed five people.

CBR weapons have been little used so far, largely due to the difficulty of obtaining the materials and the complexity of using them effectively. Where terrorists have tried to carry out CBR attacks, they have generally employed relatively simple materials. However, Al Qaeda and related groups have expressed a serious interest in using CBR. The impact of any terrorist CBR attack would depend on the success of the chosen dissemination method and the weather conditions at the time of the attack. The likelihood of a CBR attack remains low. As with other terrorist attacks, there may be no prior warning and the exact nature of an incident may not be immediately obvious. First indicators may be the sudden appearance of powders, liquids or strange smells in a building, with or without an immediate effect on people.

Good general physical and personnel security measures will contribute towards resilience against CBR incidents. Remember to apply appropriate personnel security standards to contractors, especially those with frequent access to your site.

The role of the security officer

General points include:

- review the physical security of air conditioning systems, such as access to intakes and outlets;

- restrict access to water tanks and other key utilities;

- review the security of food and drink supply chains;

- consider whether special arrangements need to be put in place for mail or parcels, such as a separate post room.

The Home Office currently advises organisations against the use of CBR detection technologies as part of their contingency planning measures. This is because the technology is not yet proven in civil settings and, in the event of a CBR incident, the emergency services would come on scene with appropriate detectors and advise accordingly. A basic awareness of the CBR threat and hazards, combined with general protective security measures – such as the screening of visitors, use of CCTV monitoring of perimeter and entrance areas and being alert to suspicious letters and packages – should offer a good level of resilience.

Consider how to communicate necessary safety advice to staff and how to offer reassurance. This needs to include instructions for those who want to enter, leave or return to a building. The local police force will be able to offer free advice on CBR protection.

CBR materials in the post

Terrorists may seek to use CBR materials in letter bombs. It is difficult to provide a full list of possible CBR indicators because of the diverse nature of the materials, but some of the more common and obvious are:

- Unexpected granular, crystalline or finely powdered material of any colour and usually with the consistency of coffee, sugar or baking powder that is loose or in a container. CBR devices containing finely ground powder or liquid may be hazardous without being opened.

- Unexpected sticky substances, sprays or vapours.
- Unexpected pieces of metal or plastic, such as discs, rods, small sheets or spheres.
- Strange smells – for example, garlicky, fishy, fruity, mothballs, peppery, meaty or rotten. If you detect a smell, do not go on sniffing it. However, some CBR materials are odourless and tasteless.
- Stains or dampness on the packaging.
- Sudden onset of illness or irritation of skin, eyes or nose.

What to do in a CBR incident

- The precise nature of the incident may not be readily apparent. Keep response plans general and wait for expert help from the emergency services.
- Be the catalyst for reviewing plans for protecting staff in the event of a terrorist threat or attack. Remember that evacuation may not be the best solution. You will need to be guided by the emergency services on the day.
- Plan for the shutdown of systems that may contribute to the movement of airborne hazards (for example, computer equipment containing fans).
- Ensure that doors can be closed quickly if required.
- If your external windows are not permanently sealed shut, develop plans for closing them in response to a warning or incident.
- Examine the feasibility of emergency shutdown of air conditioning systems and ensure that any such plans are well rehearsed.
- Where a hazard can be isolated by leaving the immediate area, do so as quickly as possible, closing doors and windows as you go.
- Move those directly affected by an incident to a safe location as close as possible to the scene of the incident, so as to minimise the spread of contamination.
- Separate those directly affected by an incident from those not involved so as to minimise the risk of inadvertent cross-contamination.

- Ask people not to wander off. Remember though that you cannot contain them against their will.

- Use your first aid skills until the emergency services arrive.

HOAX CALLS, LETTER BOMBS AND OTHER EXPLOSIVE DEVICES

Hoax bomb threat calls are designed to create alarm and disruption. They are considerably more numerous than actual incidents that have personal injury or damage as their objective. The security role is to deal with such calls calmly and efficiently so as to minimise the risk and anxiety to employees while safeguarding the company's interests. Companies must have policies and procedures for dealing with hoax calls with which security must comply. Telephone operators must be instructed on how to deal with such calls, and often this will include the transfer of the calls to trained security staff. Hoaxers can be prosecuted under Section 51 of the Criminal Law Act 1977 for placing or sending articles with the intention of inducing others to think they are bombs, or by communicating bomb threats knowing them to be false. The penalty implies a power of arrest.

Bomb threat calls

The following procedure is suggested:

- let the caller finish the message uninterrupted;
- try to write down the message exactly as the caller says it;
- if possible tie someone else into the conversation;
- ask the caller where the device has been put;
- ask what time it is due to go off;
- ask why it has been so placed;
- ask when and how it was done;
- ask for the caller's name and any code word;
- ensure that whoever in senior management is nominated in the company's instructions is told the exact contents of the call as soon as possible.

To ensure that all details required in connection with the conversation are obtained, use a pro forma. The longer the caller can be kept talking the better, and the following guidelines are suggested:

- Make it obvious you are listening.

- If any indication is shown of a grievance towards the firm or an individual, try to develop the theme; this may give a clue as to identity.

- Try to make the caller be precise about the placing and timing of the device. Probe as to why the call is being made.

- Try to provoke the caller to say more than is intended, using disbelief and even ridicule. Ask the caller what they expect you to do about it. The longer the caller talks, the more likely they are to say something unguarded. Your impressions of the call are most important, and may be the only guide management has regarding a decision about evacuation.

In a bomb threat or hoax bomb situation, management has three possible courses of action:

1. To evacuate the premises and search before allowing re-entry.
2. To search the premises without evacuation.
3. To ignore the warning.

In coming to a decision, management will need to bear in mind the following factors:

- The nature of the call.

- Whether there have been similar calls locally against a like company or product (such as those involving products tested on animals).

- Any industrial tension caused by labour disputes or strikes that may lead to someone wanting to disrupt normal working.

- The implications and dangers of any stoppage or process shutdown.

- Company policy.

- Police advice. Security may in any case be asked to inform the police and fire authorities immediately, and to notify adjoining premises.

Searching

Any search will involve company employees, including security, because the police, unfamiliar with buildings or their likely contents, cannot be expected to carry this out. Bombs and incendiary devices take many forms. Almost any item could be used, from something as large as a dustbin to as small as a cigarette packet. Any search must be methodical and carried out area by area to ensure that the whole site is covered. Companies should appoint a coordinator to oversee all the procedures once a threat has been received.

Unaccounted for or suspect objects must not be interfered with, and when such an object is found the police must be advised. When they arrive they will initiate any necessary action. The areas most likely to be affected by the leaving of bombs are those immediately adjacent to access points to the building. Unfamiliar cars should be regarded as suspect.

The use of incendiary devices is increasing, and they can be as small as a packet of cigarettes. In retail premises they may be deposited in pockets in garments, down the side of soft furnishings and so on.

The advice of the police must be sought when establishing a safe distance from any suspect device. The safe distance will depend on the size of the device and the estimated amount of explosive it might be expected to contain.

Evacuation

In an evacuation, in order to assist searching, persons must be instructed to take with them any personal belongings, bags and other articles. If there is time after the warning, there should be a search of the area concerned before evacuation. Similar action should be taken after the time limit has elapsed before re-entry of staff is allowed.

The duty to set up effective procedures is imposed on employers by Section 7 of the Management of Health and Safety at Work Regulations 1992 Code of Practice. 'In the event of serious or imminent danger', which would include fire, chemical escape, bomb threats and so on, the legislation requires the 'nomination of a sufficient number of competent persons to implement procedures insofar as they relate to the evacuation from the premises of people at work' and makes clear that they should not return where danger remains. A 'competent person' is defined as 'one with sufficient training, experience or knowledge to enable that person to implement the evacuation action'.

A companion code states: 'These Regulations apply to a very wide range of workplaces not only factories, shops and offices but, for example, schools, hospitals, hotels and places of entertainment'. Section 4 of the Health and Safety at Work Act 1974 carries managerial responsibilities beyond employees to include visitors, clients, customers and shoppers.

Security officers are certain to be involved in any evacuation and should at the very least have printed instructions with which they should be conversant. In the case of an evacuation from retail premises where there is always a danger of panic, security staff and management must be seen to be acting with total calm and confidence.

Letter bombs

These are contained in envelopes and parcels and may be delivered either by courier or through the normal postal services. They are often in the form of a flat, padded letter weighing about 4 ounces or a parcel the size of a book. In the course of normal handling they may not be dangerous, but immediately become so when an attempt is made to open them.

If the security department is expected to deal with incoming mail, the following traits may make an unfamiliar object appear suspect:

- A foreign or unfamiliar postmark.

- Writing that is foreign or that lacks literacy or legibility, or that is crudely printed.

- Letters labelled 'personal' or 'private' that are addressed to senior management but under the job title such as 'The Managing Director'.

- The address of the sender shown on the flap does not tally with the postmark.

- Excessive weight for the size of the package and apparent contents.

- Uneven weight distribution (which may indicate the presence of batteries).

- Visible grease marks on the outer packaging (which may indicate 'sweating' explosive).

- The smell of marzipan or almonds.

- Excessive or abnormal fastening for the type of package; the outer envelope may contain an inner wrapping in the form of a booby trap.

- Parcels or envelopes that rattle, feel springy or are damaged, giving sight of wire, batteries or fuel-filled sachets.

These are cumulative points that may give rise to increasing degrees of suspicion. If the letter or package cannot be accounted for then the following procedure must be adopted:

- Do not try to open the package or letter, or tamper with it unnecessarily.

- Do not place it in water or put anything on top of it.

- Isolate it to a place where it can do minimum harm. Use minimum handling, placing it in a locked room, say in a nest of sandbags, but leaving it so that it can be visually inspected with ease.

- Keep people away from the letter or package, and open windows and doors in the vicinity.

- Inform the police, giving them full details of the letter or package, its markings and any peculiarities that have given rise to suspicion.

Equipment is available that will enable letters and packages to be screened before they are opened. Up to the time of writing, no explosive packets have been received that did not contain metal in some form or other.

CRIME AND INCIDENT SCENE PRESERVATION

The protection of a crime scene is critical in the investigation of crime by the police. It is important that security staff recognise this and implement the following procedures once a crime scene has been discovered:

- inform someone else about the crime and the scene;

- get assistance;

- call the police;

- cordon off the area and, where possible, lock any entrance to the crime scene;

- move away onlookers who are not witnesses;

- avoid speaking to anyone from the media about the incident;

- do not touch anything within the crime scene;

- enter the scene only to save life or to render emergency first aid;

- do not let anyone other than the police enter the crime scene, including any other employees or management;

- obtain details of any witnesses to the crime or incident who cannot remain at the scene until the police arrive;

- remain vigilant to other connected or unconnected incidents;

- give assistance to the police, including access to any CCTV footage of the incident;

- write down your recollection of the incident and what you did as soon as possible afterwards.

20 First Aid

The Health and Safety (First Aid) Regulations 1981 require employers to provide adequate and appropriate equipment, facilities and personnel to render first aid treatment to injured or ill employees at work. The persons appointed as first aiders will not be acceptable unless qualified by approved training and examination and holders of current certificates to that effect.

Pre-eminent training and examining bodies at the moment are St John and St Andrew Ambulance Associations and the British Red Cross, all of whom hold frequent courses in all parts of the country. Certificate validity is three years, after which a refresher course and further examinations are needed.

The wearer of a uniform is automatically looked to for assistance in emergencies, and first aid responsibilities fit in well with security duties. Even if the job being done does not require this competence, there are important advantages in having the first aid qualification: particularly in the case of contract security, the ability to administer first aid will enhance the value and extent of the service which can be offered and, for the individual, will represent a distinct asset when seeking employment.

BASIC FIRST AID

Although there is no substitute for recognised training, there are some basic principles of first aid that everybody should know about. The following are examples:

- *Prevent further injury.* Remove the source of injury or remove the casualty from the source; for example, switch off electricity, stop machinery, drag the casualty from fire, carry them from a gas-filled room and so on.

- *Preserve life*. If breathing has stopped give artificial respiration. If pulse has stopped perform external chest compression. Control serious bleeding.

- *Prevent the condition from becoming worse*. With serious injuries, do not move the casualty unless it is necessary to do so to prevent further damage.

- *Send for assistance*. Give an indication of the extent of the injuries and condition of the casualty as well as the precise location and the quickest way to get there.

- *Alleviate pain*. With the minimum of movement, get the casualty into the most comfortable resting position. Reassure the casualty in a confident manner and try to find out what happened if the cause is not self-evident.

- *Minimise shock effect*. Keep the casualty warm without over-heating. Loosen tight clothing and reassure the casualty.

- *Obtain history and assist skilled help*. Obtain all the information you can about the cause of the injury from the casualty or witnesses. Note anything the casualty says about symptoms and watch for changes in their condition. Give all this information to those who are removing the casualty.

- *Be cautious, calm and authoritative*. In particular: (a) do not attempt too much or usurp the function of a doctor; (b) remove no more clothing than is absolutely necessary; (c) disperse any crowd that gathers; (d) maintain a reassuring manner and avoid any impression of being alarmed or agitated.

- *Persevere*. If the casualty appears to be dead but there is the slightest doubt about this, continue treatment (if necessary with the assistance of helpers acting under your directions) until medical aid takes over or the stiffening of muscles indicates that death is definite.

LEVELS OF CONSCIOUSNESS

There are different degrees of consciousness:

- *Full consciousness* – self explanatory.

- *Drowsiness* – meaning the casualty is easily aroused but lapses into unconsciousness.

- *Stupor* – unconsciousness from which the casualty can be aroused with difficulty in so far as the casualty is aware of a stimulus in the form of a nip or pinch, but does not comprehend what is being said.

- *Coma* – the casualty cannot be aroused at all.

Almost always, unconsciousness is serious, and the cause of it might not be obvious at first sight. Common sources of loss of consciousness are:

- acute shock

- skull fracture

- compression of the brain or concussion

- heavy bleeding

- epilepsy

- diabetes and insulin coma

- fainting

- asphyxia and its various causes

- stroke

- infantile convulsion

- heart attack

- poisoning.

Where there are no visible injuries, diagnosis depends on powers of observation. Always check the casualty's pockets to see whether a card is being carried that would indicate that the casualty is undergoing medical treatment and that might show the reason for the collapse and indicate the required treatment. Examples are cards indicating diabetes, steroid use (cortisone-taking) and anti-coagulant drugs to prevent blood-clotting.

Diabetic casualties are a special and frequent category that may be quickly recognised. Unconsciousness in a diabetic is caused by the casualty having taken too little or too much insulin. An overdose of insulin causes profuse sweating, rapid pulse and shallow breathing. If there is a spasm of consciousness, induce the subject to swallow sugar in any form. Otherwise, get medical assistance at once.

Epileptics in major fits can seem to be more seriously ill than they really are. The face and neck become congested and livid; the body rigid at first and then convulsive; frothing at the mouth occurs. Finally, the casualty becomes totally relaxed and recovers consciousness with little ill effect. The main concern is keeping the casualty from further injury by self-harm or injury from other sources.

DEALING WITH AN UNCONSCIOUS CASUALTY

1. Remove from other sources of danger.
2. To establish the degree of unconsciousness, ask a question and give a command in order to gauge the response. Shake the casualty. Also: (a) Open the airway, place two fingers on the casualty's chin and one hand on their forehead. Tilt the head and lift the chin. (b) Listen, feel and look at the chest for signs of breathing. (c) Turn the casualty into the recovery position for 10 seconds. (d) Check the carotid pulse in the neck for 10 seconds.
3. Check the casualty from head to toe for external bleeding.
4. Re-check breathing and pulse.
5. Send or go for help.

Recovery position

1. Kneel beside the casualty.
2. Straighten legs.
3. Place near arm out at right angle to shoulder.
4. Bend elbow (policeman 'stop' position).
5. Place far arm across chest.
6. Hold your hand against the cheek nearest to you.
7. Grasp the far thigh.
8. Pull far knee up, foot flat on floor.
9. Roll casualty on to lap.
10. Adjust upper leg to right angle to body.
11. Adjust position of chin and head if necessary.

RESUSCITATION

Mouth-to-mouth ventilation

With the casualty in the position where the airway is open, check for:

- **D**anger
- **R**esponse
- **A**irway
- **B**reathing.

Then send for help.

Give two ventilations using the following format:

1. Open your mouth wide and take a deep breath.

2. Pinch the casualty's nostrils together to prevent air leakage.

3. Seal your lips around the casualty's mouth.

4. Blow into the casualty's mouth until the lungs are filled and the chest rises (two seconds).

5. Lift off from mouth, listen for exhaled air and watch for chest movement (four seconds).

Then:

- check pulse;

- if pulse present, continue with ten ventilations;

- check pulse for ten seconds;

- if pulse present, continue with ten ventilations;

- check pulse after every ten ventilations (one minute);

- continue until help arrives.

External chest compression method

This is essentially a task for a *trained* first aider. The procedure is:

1. Lay the casualty flat on their back on a firm surface.

2. Kneel beside and facing the casualty, level with the casualty's heart.

3. Place the heel of one hand on the breast bone, about two finger widths above where the rib margins join at its bottom. Place the heel of the other hand on the top of that one and interlock the fingers, avoiding pressure on the ribs.

4. Adjust your position so that your arms are straight and positioned vertically over the breastbone.

5. Press vertically down on the lower half of breastbone to move it 4–5 centimetres (1.5–2 inches) and then relax the pressure, which should be applied firmly and smoothly. Repeat the compression and release sequence at the rate of 100 per minute. Use the same rate for children, but using one hand and lighter pressure.

6. With one first aider present there should be at least 30 heart compressions followed by two mouth-to-mouth inflations, the

sequence being repeated. In the case of a child, five compressions followed by one ventilation.

External chest compressions combined with mouth-to-mouth ventilation is known as CPR (cardio pulmonary resuscitation).

BLEEDING

Excessive bleeding from any of the main blood vessels, either *internal* or *external*, will endanger life unless it is quickly stopped. The signs and symptoms of both types of bleeding are similar but, in the case of internal bleeding their cause may not be obvious at once.

Internal bleeding

Symptoms of internal bleeding are:

- pale appearance;
- cold and clammy skin;
- weak rapid pulse;
- complaint of pain, feeling faint, dizziness and nausea;
- shallow gasping breathing, which may be accompanied by yawning and sighing;
- restlessness and excitability, coupled with complaints of being thirsty;
- developing lassitude and apathy;
- the facts about how the injury was sustained.

Internal bleeding may appear in a variety of ways, which will give some indication as to the damage to organs.

- *Fractured skull* – blood issuing from the ear canal or nose, or appearing as a 'blood-shot' eye.
- *Lungs* – bright red, frothy blood which is coughed up.
- *Stomach* – vomit that is bright red or that resembles coffee grounds.

In the case of internal bleeding, loosen all tight clothing and move the casualty into a position of absolute rest, with their legs raised and as comfortable as possible. Send for immediate medical aid and an ambulance and keep the casualty warm and relaxed. If conscious, reassure the casualty and try to get them to relax physically and mentally, keeping a careful watch on their pulse and breathing. Do not give the casualty anything to drink.

External bleeding

Lay the casualty down, with raised legs if possible:

1.   Apply pressure directly over the wound. If the wound area is large try to press the sides of the wound together. However, where there is a foreign body within a wound that cannot be removed without further risk to the casualty, *do not attempt to remove it.* Avoid pressure on it until medical advice is given. If a broken bone protrudes, as far as possible avoid all pressure directly on it.

2.   If a dressing is available, apply it directly over the wound, press it down and bandage it firmly.

3.   If bleeding does not stop, continue to apply dressings and bandage more firmly.

4.   Raise the injured part and support it in position, unless the wound is accompanied by a fracture.

5.   If direct pressure does not stop the bleeding, or when such pressure cannot be applied, indirect pressure should be applied at the nearest pressure point to the wound between the wound and the heart. These are places where an artery can be compressed against a bone so as to flatten it and stop the flow of blood. The brachial artery on the inner side of the upper arm and femoral artery in the groin can control major blood loss. This can be done while dressings are being prepared for direct application, and should not be continued longer than 10 minutes.

6.   Get skilled assistance. Keep the casualty warm to minimise shock and ensure removal to hospital as soon as possible.

7.   Do not plug or otherwise try to stop the flow of blood from the ear – cover with a sterilised dressing. Bleeding from the ear may be indicative of a fractured skull in which an internal pressure build-up must be avoided.

BROKEN BONES

The following first aid treatment is required:

•   maintain an open airway;

- leave the casualty in the position found, unless in any danger;
- do not attempt to move broken bones;
- steady and support the injured part, if possible;
- provide more permanent support with padding;
- obtain appropriate medical treatment.

HEAD INJURIES

There is usually external evidence of head injury. Symptoms include:

- subject may be dazed or unconscious;
- bleeding from the nose, mouth or ears;
- pupils of eyes might be a different size;
- one or more extremities on one side of the body may be paralysed;
- breathing sometimes becomes noisy and perhaps bubbly;
- in serious cases, body temperature may rise and the pulse may become slow.

With head injuries, extreme care should be taken when bandaging wounds. No pressure must be placed on the skull. If the casualty has been unconscious at all, even with a minor head injury, they should be taken to hospital.

Do not forget when at the scene that almost all criminal attacks result in head injuries. Look out for possible weapons, witnesses or anything that might have a bearing on the cause of the injury.

MAJOR BURNS AND SCALDS

The following first aid treatment is required:

- remove the casualty from the danger area;
- if clothing is on fire, put it out by wrapping around a blanket, coat or anything handy that will exclude air (but do not use nylon or similar materials);
- cool the affected area with cold water for at least 10 minutes to lessen the pain and reduce heat in the tissues;
- remove anything restrictive on the affected area such as boots, belts and so on, but do not attempt to remove any clothing that may possibly be sticking to a burn;

- reassure the casualty;
- arrange immediate removal to hospital.

Do not:

- apply any lotions, ointments or oil dressings;
- break blisters;
- do anything that will increase the risk of infection to the burnt area.

Burnt areas may be covered by dressings or sheets, but these must be as clean as possible so as to avoid infection.

Where corrosive chemicals have caused the burns:

- flood the area for at least 20 minutes with water but avoid being affected yourself;
- if possible, remove any contaminated clothing from the injured area while carrying out the flooding;
- flooding is especially important where there is a risk of eye injury from the chemicals concerned.

POISONING

This is hard to diagnose if the casualty is unconscious. If poisoning is suspected, care must be taken when applying mouth-to-mouth resuscitation. If mouth-to-mouth ventilation is essential, use a plastic face shield or blow through a handkerchief after wiping the casualty's mouth. If the casualty is conscious, quickly ask what has been taken, remembering that the casualty may lose consciousness at any time.

Corrosive poisons may burn the mouth and lips; if such burns are present the first aider must not induce vomiting but give the casualty frequent sips of water or milk.

If the casualty is unconscious, administer the general treatment as described earlier, and in all cases ensure removal to hospital as soon as possible, either by car or by ambulance. Look for and retain anything that may be connected with the poisoning, such as bottles, pills and cartons, and obtain a sample of any vomit excreted by the casualty. These must all be taken to hospital with the casualty, together with any other information that may be of assistance to the doctors.

HEART ATTACKS

The most common forms of heart attack are angina and coronary thrombosis.

Angina is caused by a narrowing of the arteries and its most common symptom is where pain radiates down the inner side of the arm that may affect the throat and jaws.

Coronary thrombosis is caused by a clot of blood blocking a coronary artery, giving rise to severe pain behind the breastbone, which may radiate down the arms. Other symptoms are:

- cold sweat
- rapid pulse
- shortness of breath.

  The first aid to be applied is as follows:

- Put the casualty in the most comfortable position that suits them, probably half-sitting with head and shoulders raised; sitting on the floor with their back to the wall has been recommended.
- Loosen all tight clothing.
- Reassure the casualty.
- Move the casualty as little as possible.

  In angina cases, the casualty may take their own medicine.

SHOCK

Shock is the state of collapse associated with severe injury both internal and external. If not treated it can lead to death. The symptoms are:

- feeling faint or giddy
- swimming vision
- facial pallor
- sweating
- cold and clammy skin
- shallow and rapid breathing, becoming gasping
- increased pulse rate with the pulse weakening.

The first aid to be applied is as follows:

- Treat the original injury and waste no time in removing the casualty to hospital.
- Loosen any clothing at the neck, chest and waist.
- Lay the casualty down, with raised legs.
- Do not move the casualty any more than is essential.
- Keep the casualty warm but not hot.
- Do not give the casualty anything to drink.
- If the casualty complains of thirst, moisten the lips only.

21 Conflict Resolution

Every year in England and Wales over half a million workers suffer personal injury as a result of violent incidents at work. Before dealing with the nuts and bolts of personal safety practice, it is appropriate to outline the legal obligations imposed on employers and employees in respect of both security and safety responsibilities in the workplace.

Protection against violence is an obvious obligation and this can be helped by recognition of the behavioural symptoms that lead up to it. Knowledge of these can help a security officer diffuse an impending incident, and help condition his or her response to the individuals involved.

The principal legislation covering health and safety in the workplace in the United Kingdom is the Health and Safety at Work Act 1974. The Act places a legal obligation on employers to ensure, so far as is reasonably practicable, the health, safety and welfare of their employees at work. The Act also states that it is an employer's duty to provide such information, training and supervision as is necessary to ensure the health, safety and welfare of employees.

In the past, the Health and Safety at Work Act and its accompanying legislation have sometimes been misinterpreted as being directed solely for the protection of people involved in manual work, such as in the construction trades or the manufacture or distribution of hazardous substances. This is not the case. The legislation is designed to protect all employees, including those who work in the so-called 'white collar' industries where workplace risks might centre on their interactions with other people and involve issues like personal physical violence, threats of violence, psychological abuse, intimidation and harassment. The health and safety legislation also protects those who might be termed 'lone workers', such as company representatives, employed away from a centralised workplace.

VIOLENCE AND RISK

The Health and Safety Executive defines violence at work as:

> *Any incident in which an employee is abused, threatened or assaulted by any person in circumstances arising out of their work. This can include verbal abuse and threats as well as physical assault.*

Under the Management of Health and Safety at Work Regulations 1992, an employer has a legal obligation to identify the risks that their employees are exposed to at work and those that might reasonably be foreseen. This includes assessment of the risks of violence in the workplace. (Chapter 17 includes more information about risk assessment.)

REPORTING INCIDENTS

Central to staying safe and ensuring procedures are reviewed and updated is the reporting to employers of incidents of personal violence. The wide definition of violence means that many incidents and occurrences affecting an employee's ability to work without fear of personal violence could be reported, but willingness to report incidents is often inhibited by cumbersome reporting procedures and differences in where people draw the line between acceptable and unacceptable conduct. Personal violence is a personal thing. Violence to some might mean physical assault; to others it might mean verbal or psychological abuse, the threat of violence, bullying, intimidation or harassment.

Health and safety legislation also states that we as individuals have a legal responsibility for the safety of our colleagues. Here, the question to be addressed might be: 'If an incident or occurrence is not reported, might others be put at risk from a similar incident or occurrence in the future?' However, there are other factors that will influence the need to report incidents and occurrences, including: (a) that data collected from the recording of incidents and occurrences will provide an accurate overview of risk; and (b) that the data collected will assist management in carrying out a risk assessment and producing a workable personal safety policy that will include strategies and guidelines to enhance safety and reduce the potential for personal injury.

It is worth noting here that under Section 7a of the Health and Safety at Work Act 1974 a duty is imposed on employees while at work to take reasonable care for the health and safety of themselves and of other persons who may be affected by their acts or omissions at work. Therefore, failing to report a violent incident or occurrence that might affect others in future could be in breach of this law.

The remainder of this chapter will address the following issues:

- the risks of violence in perspective;
- assessing body language to identify threats;
- warning and danger signs;
- understanding intuition;
- communication models;
- barriers to communication;
- impact factors;
- personal space;
- diffusing aggression;
- planning for safety when out and about on patrol;
- the law in relation to the use of force, self-defence and offensive weapons.

THE RISKS OF VIOLENCE IN PERSPECTIVE

Statistics in Home Office *Crime in England and Wales 2005/06* statistical bulletin suggest that almost one in six of crimes recorded by the police include violence of some sort. There is no doubt that these 'national figures' are inflated by the violence experienced in our major cities, and that in some areas of England and Wales the violence is involved in no more than four per 100 crimes recorded.

Our perceptions of violence and therefore our risk is influenced by a number of things, including:

- personal experience of being a victim;
- knowledge of someone who has been a victim;
- the media and television portrayal and reporting of violence;
- where we live;
- where we work;
- the type of job we do;
- our social habits.

The type of job we do greatly influences our risk of violence, but there is no current research suggesting that security personnel are at greater risk of violence than any other profession outside of the health service, teaching and the police. Also, there is a high clear-up rate of violence offences (as much as 90 per cent in some areas), suggesting that the majority of violence offences, and sexual ones for that matter, are committed by people on people that they know. The risk of being a victim of indiscriminate violence from a complete stranger is very low indeed. Risk of violence can further be reduced by the way we influence opportunity. This may be done by:

- Adjusting our social habits so that we avoid known trouble or violence spots.

- Assessing the need to carry out tasks or make journeys at certain times of day that are perceived to be risky.

- Increasing staffing levels, particularly in working environments where the risk of attack is increased because of the high value of goods kept on premises or being transported.

- A commitment to regular staff training in anger management, assertiveness and tactical techniques.

ASSESSING BODY LANGUAGE TO IDENTIFY THREATS

Body language can be described as 'an unconscious language that communicates feelings and attitudes without words'. Our first impressions of people are vital to staying safe. How we deal with a person, or our expectations of them, are influenced by a variety of characteristics, including:

- how they look;

- what they wear;

- their facial expressions;

- their mannerisms.

Our initial perceptions of people might be right or wrong and may change the longer we interact with them. Some perceptions, though, are based upon prejudices and assumptions that have little bearing on reality.

Warning signs

Warning signs indicate that a person is getting angry and that they feel they have to verbally exert their presence. Warning signs may include:

- direct, prolonged eye contact;
- facial colour may darken;
- head is back;
- subject stands tall;
- kicking the ground;
- large body movements close to people;
- breathing rate accelerates;
- behaviour may stop or start abruptly.

Danger signs

Danger signs are the body's natural reactions to the possibility of physical contact. These signs may include:

- fists clenching and unclenching;
- facial colour may become paler;
- lips tighten over teeth;
- head drops to protect throat;
- eyebrows droop to protect eyes;
- hands are raised above the waist;
- shoulders become tense;
- stance moves from square to sideways;
- the stare is directed towards the intended target;
- there is a lowering of the body to launch forward.

Coupled with our use of intuition (discussed next), these warning and danger signs should enable us to stay clear of the threat, inform others of the threat and get assistance to counter or deal with the threat *before* we get involved.

It must also be remembered that a person's aggression may be greatly influenced by other factors, including:

- the need to escape for fear of apprehension and detention;

- whether they are under the influence of drugs or alcohol;
- their psychological or mental state;
- whether they have a physical disability that causes them frustration;
- whether they are ill;
- whether they are the victim of some other social frustration such as being unemployed, having no money or suffering from marital problems.

INTUITION

Everyday, we all get certain 'gut feelings' about people and a whole range of situations. For example, many of us at some time in our lives have felt that we were being followed: this, for some, will have created an unease that triggers breathlessness, an increase in heartbeat, becoming cold or clammy, shaking, the mind racing and so on. These natural responses can cloud our ability to make positive decisions about staying safe, but they are responses that indicate to us that something about a person or situation has put us on our guard. These responses can quickly be dissipated by removing ourselves from the worrying situation to a place we know to be safe. Ignoring our intuition may increase the possibility of us becoming a victim.

Our intuition is driven by 'messengers', that put us into a state of alert. The messengers of intuition include:

- gut feelings
- nagging thoughts
- apprehension
- anxiety
- wonder
- suspicion
- hesitation
- doubt
- fear.

We must continually question our intuition before proceeding 'where people fear to tread'. We must get into the habit of asking ourselves 'Why have I got these feelings?' and then reacting to them by doing something else or by getting assistance. Here are some relevant statements that work alongside intuition:

- The fact that you fear or worry about something is sound evidence that personal danger is not imminent. While you are worrying about something happening, it is *not* actually happening.
- True fear is a signal that only sounds in the presence of immediate danger.
- Where you feel fear, listen.
- When you do not feel fear, do not manufacture it.
- If you feel worried, ask yourself why?

CONFLICT RESOLUTION COMMUNICATION MODELS

There are two communication models recognised in conflict resolution training. These are described using the acronyms LEAPS and CUDSA.

LEAPS

- **L** = Listen – Listen carefully to what is being said; this may disguise the nature of the problem.
- **E** = Empathise – Use examples from your experience to show that you comprehend what is being said. This will show that you can relate to the speaker.
- **A** = Ask questions – Ask the speaker questions as this will show that you are seeking to identify the source of the conflict.
- **P** = Paraphrase – Repeat what is being said to show understanding and to satisfy yourself and the speaker that you have a grasp of the problem.
- **S** = Summarise – Give a summary of what the speaker has said, ensuring that key points have been understood.

CUDSA

This is another form of communication that is suitable when dealing specifically with conflict resolution.

- **C** = Confront the conflict, acknowledging that there is conflict and that you want to resolve it.

- **U** = Understand each other's position, making clear statements about your own position and listening actively to the other person to clarify positions and diffuse emotions.

- **D** = Define the problem, ensuring that both of you agree about the definition and accept that both of you will need to give ground to change the position.

- **S** = Search for and evaluate alternative solutions, mutually generating possible alternatives, and making trade-offs and compromises.

- **A** = Agree upon and implement the best solution.

SKILLS AND APPROACHES TO CONFLICT

Each of the stages of CUDSA involves the use of specific skills. When confronting conflict you need to:

- keep calm;

- be assertive, rather than passive or aggressive;

- emphasise that you are looking for a solution through collaboration;

- express feelings and wishes assertively;

- focus on the issues;

- admit to, and alter misconceptions;

- focus on areas of common ground;

- make trade-offs and compromises;

- ask questions to check and clarify facts, opinions and wishes.

Barriers to communication

There are many barriers to communication. Here are some:

- prejudice;

- ignorance;

- lack of understanding;

- our body language;

- language – the speaker may not speak English very well.

IMPACT FACTORS

Impact factors must be identified when dealing with conflict. We must assess both our own impact factors – for example, are we contributing to the conflict? – and those of the other person, such as whether they are tall, appear fit and healthy, and are well built. If the situation became physical, could you handle it?

Impact factors to consider include:

- sex, age and size;
- relative strength;
- skill level – such as experience of self-defence techniques;
- specialist knowledge;
- alcohol or drugs;
- mental illness;
- being in a position of disadvantage;
- injury or exhaustion;
- imminent danger;
- numbers present;
- weapons.

People desperately in need of drugs to satisfy their habit may become violent. In this instance, assistance from colleagues may be necessary. The same is possible with people who have mental health problems; therefore, in a hospital environment, the help of specialist staff may be needed.

PERSONAL SPACE

Distance gives us time to think and then react. We naturally allow some people closer and we give others a wide berth. However, we sometimes might not have that luxury. We have to consider what safe distances are because they are critical in preserving our personal safety and the safety of others. There are three zones to consider:

- danger zone
- personal zone
- aware zone.

Danger zone

The danger zone is illustrated in Figure 21.1. This is where violence is

imminent and likely. In these circumstances it is important to move to a 'reaction gap' – the distance between the extremities of your reach and the extremities of your opponent's reach. Their reach includes any weapons they might have.

6 to 18 inches

What you can't see!

Figure 21.1 Danger zone

Personal zone

This zone usually relates to a distance kept between friends and associates

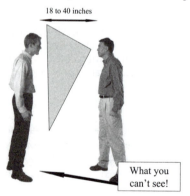

who present no threat of violence (see Figure 21.2). In conflict situations this distance is still within what is to be considered the reaction gap.

18 to 40 inches

What you can't see!

Figure 21.2 Personal zone

Aware zone

The aware zone (see Figure 21.3) is considered to be the minimum safe distance when dealing with someone who is aggressive and likely to be physically violent. This distance is also described as the reaction gap.

40 inches to 10 feet

Figure 21.3 Aware zone

DIFFUSING AGGRESSION

Careful management of an aggressive situation by calming and relating to the needs of the aggressor may result in a positive and satisfactory outcome.

When dealing with conflict, remember that 'If you remove logs from a fire, the fire goes out', and consider the following:

- Remain calm. If you are not in control they are.

- Use calming body language. Eventually the aggressor will match yours. If you get aggressive so will they.

- Speak slowly and calmly.

- Listen carefully to what is being said before attempting to solve the problem. It is usual for the speaker to indicate a likely solution by what they say.

- Look for a positive outcome instead of trying to sort out the person's attitude.

- Let personal insults wash over you in the interest of gaining a positive outcome.

- Always anticipate violence.

The following points are also worthy of note:

- We do not have any control over the way others behave, but we do have control over ourselves.

- The calmer we remain, the less reason the other person will have for continuing with their behaviour.

In addition, a method of changing the balance of control is to ask questions. A simple question of an aggressive person such as 'Are you going to assault me?' might prompt the aggressor to calm down. Likewise, a sudden reaction that is unexpected might confuse the aggressor and prompt them to move away. For example, a man was walking in a street late at night. The street was well-lit but there was no one else about. He was suddenly confronted by a masked man with a knife who demanded his wallet. The victim threw the wallet onto the pavement. This was totally unexpected for the assailant who, it was guessed, was used to wallets being handed over. The assailant turned and ran leaving the wallet on the pavement. It is assumed that the assailant made off because of his uncertainty about the results of picking the wallet up off the pavement.

PLANNING FOR SAFETY WHEN PATROLLING ON FOOT

Prior planning prevents poor performance and significantly decreases the risk of being a victim of violence. Familiarity and complacency are the biggest obstacles to staying safe.

Preparation

- Wear sensible clothing and footwear, especially if it is issued for the purpose of enhancing personal safety.

- Familiarise yourself with the location of your work. Get to know the surroundings.

- Tell other people of your movements and keep people informed of changes to your routine.

- Try not to wear loose items like scarves that could be grabbed or used to cause personal injury.

- Know where help is. Get to know avenues of escape and so on.

While on patrol

- Look confident, walk purposefully at a good pace. This will exude purpose, organisation and authority.

- Try to keep at least one hand free – both if possible.

- Vary the patrol route.

- Follow your intuition. If it is compromised get help. Do not proceed.

- Remain alert at all times and report all incidents. Remember your legal obligations towards colleagues.

- Never assume that violence will not happen to you.

USE OF FORCE

It is good law and good sense that a person who is being attacked has the right to defend themselves. Indeed the Magna Carta of 1215 gave us all the right to defend ourselves, our family and our property. Common law includes a person's right to defend himself and others, but the principal statute law is to be found in Section 3(1) of the Criminal Law Act 1967:

Any person may use such force as is reasonable in the circumstances in:

a) The prevention of crime or

b) To detain or assist in the lawful detention of an offender or suspected offender or

c) A person unlawfully at large.

The key word in the definition is 'reasonable'. What is reasonable is the judgement of the person being attacked concerning that which he or she honestly and instinctively though necessary to fight off the attacker. The Crown Prosecution Service, and ultimately a magistrate or judge, will take into account the following in the assessment of whether the force used was reasonable:

- the amount force used;

- the proportionality of the force used;

- the seriousness of the crime to be prevented;

- the right of self-defence.

Positional asphyxia and the use of force in making an arrest

Positional asphyxia is a form of asphyxia that occurs when someone's position prevents them from breathing adequately. A small but significant number of people die suddenly and without apparent reason during restraint by, for example, the police, prison officers and healthcare staff. Positional asphyxia may be a factor in some of these deaths.

Research has suggested that restraining a person in a face down position is likely to cause greater restriction of breathing than restraining people face up. Almost all subjects who have died during restraint have engaged in extreme levels of physical resistance against restraint for a prolonged period of time. Other issues in the way the subject is restrained can also increase the risk of death, such as kneeling or otherwise placing weight on the subject, and particularly placing any type of restraint hold around the subject's neck. Before practising restraint it is important that the security officer has undergone approved control and restraint training.

OFFENSIVE WEAPONS

The Prevention of Crime Act 1953 is the statute law under which people are prosecuted for possessing offensive weapons. Note that the possession has to be in a public place, not on private property. Section 3 of the Act states:

> *It is an offence for any person to have with him in any public place an offensive weapon.*

An offensive weapon includes:

> *Any article made, intended or adapted for causing injury, or intended for such use; and articles carried solely to be used in self-defence.*

Examples of articles *made* might include a firearm, a cosh, a flick knife, a bayonet or a knuckle duster. 'Articles *intended*' means any article carried for the sole purpose of self-defence; this might include a rolling pin or baseball bat. *Adapted* articles might include a sharpened comb handle or car keys placed between the fingers to act as a weapon.

Possessing an offensive weapon is an indictable offence that carries a power of arrest for people other than the police (see Chapter 10).

22 Cultural and Diversity Awareness

Perceptions of people from different cultures can be driven by bigotry, misunderstanding and intolerance. These pages are designed to give a basic understanding of the different cultures that can be seen in the United Kingdom and elsewhere. In addition, the chapter looks at diversity issues that are relevant to the way we organise our lives, and the way that we manage people and situations within our lives. The text will also underpin the knowledge required to gain professional qualifications in door supervision.

Culture can be defined as a set of distinctive spiritual, material, intellectual and emotional features of society or a social group, which encompasses ways of living together, value systems, traditions and beliefs.

BASIC CULTURAL AND DIVERSITY PRINCIPLES

To demonstrate fairness and build confidence we need to:

- treat everyone with dignity and respect;
- recognise and guard against our own prejudices;
- be aware of issues that affect people from minority communities;
- be colour conscious, not colour blind.

Treating everyone in the same way may not mean that you are treating everyone fairly. For instance, holding team meetings at certain times may cause difficulty for some people whose faith requires them to practise ritual prayer at set times. Ritual prayer is an essential part of the cultural and religious beliefs of some ethnic communities and in some workplaces, multifaith prayer rooms have been set aside for those who wish to observe that religious practice.

It is important that we as individuals do not project cultural stereotypes. In some communities a lack of eye contact indicates respect, but it should not be assumed that all black and Asian people avoid eye contact for that reason. Many young black and Asian people are second and third generation British born citizens and may be no different from any other teenager when faced with authority figures.

Appropriate words

It is important that we do not use inappropriate, dated or offensive words. Some words that were once acceptable no longer are, so people must choose carefully the words they use. The following is a guide but is not to be regarded as definitive:

- *Black.* Acceptable to people of African or Caribbean origin.
- *Coloured.* An offensive term that should not be used.
- *Non-white.* Should never be used as it implies a negative value judgement.
- *Visible minorities.* Has a wider scope than black so is generally acceptable.
- *Racial minorities.* Often used as an alternative to ethnic minorities. Both are acceptable.
- *Ethnics.* A deeply offensive term.
- *Ethnic monitoring.* Acceptable when applied to systems of monitoring.
- *African Caribbean.* Preferable to West Indian or Afro-Caribbean. Young people may prefer being called black or black British.
- *African.* Acceptable as it refers to a country or continent from which a person, family or community may have originated.
- *Asian.* Should be used with care. Some people prefer to identify themselves by reference to their country of origin.
- *Half-caste.* Not acceptable. Mixed parentage is better.
- *Oriental.* Not acceptable. The country of origin should be used – for example, Chinese.
- *West Indian.* Not to be used as a generic term. It is better to refer to such people by their country of origin – for example, Jamaican.

It is just as offensive to describe other nationalities in a derogatory way, such as 'Taff', 'Jock' or 'Paddy'.

SIKH FAITH COMMUNITY AND CUSTOMS

Core beliefs

Remembering God in daily and truthful living, with service to others being particularly important and, by this, being reunited with God.

Daily acts of faith

- Rise early, bathe and meditate before morning prayers.
- Evening prayers before bed.
- Collective worship on Sundays.

Rules of life

Five articles of faith (the 'Five Ks'):

1. *Kesh – uncut hair covered by a turban.*

2. *Kangha – a comb to keep the hair tidy.*

3. *Kara – a steel bangle symbolising unity with God.*

4. *Kirpan – a short dagger symbolising readiness to fight against injustice and protect the oppressed.*

5. *Kacha – shorts to symbolise modesty.*

In addition, the articles prescribe earning an ethical living, remembering God every day, sharing with the needs of others and spending some time regularly in service with others.

Places of worship

The Sikh temple is the Gurdwara. All shoes must be removed and visitors and worshippers must perform ablutions and bow to the scriptures prior to entry. Visitors and worshippers must dress moderately, cover everything, wear a head covering and remain silent. They are to be seated on the floor with sexes separated and their legs bent underneath. Food is then blessed and served to all.

Annual events

- *Guru Nanak's Birthday.* A three-day celebration of the founder's birth.

- *The Martyrdom of Guru Tegh Bahadur.* To commemorate the death of the Guru for believing in religious freedom.

- *Guru Gobind Singh's Birthday.* A celebration of the Guru who introduced the initiation ceremony and code of discipline.

- *The Martyrdom of Guru Arjan Dev.* To commemorate the Guru who completed the work on the Golden Temple of Amritsar.

- *Baisakhri.* The replacement of the Sikh flag outside the Gurdwara.

- *Divali.* The lighting of the Gurdwara in remembrance of Guru Hargobind.

Language

The language used in the United Kingdom is mainly English, Urdu, Hindi, Swahili and Punjabi. Text is written in Gurmukhi.

Dress

- Adherence to the 'Five Ks' is paramount.
- Removal of the turban is highly embarrassing.
- Modest dress is required at all times for both sexes.

Diet

Sikhs generally refrain from eating beef, pork or halal meat and from taking alcohol, drugs and tobacco. Most tend to be vegetarians, eating dahl, rice, salads, vegetables or fruit.

Names

Sikhs usually have three names. First, the given name, then their title (Singh for a boy, meaning lion and Kaur for a girl, meaning princess) and finally a family name. Sikhs will tend to use their given name and title rather than the given and family name – for example Kulvinder Kaur or Peter Singh. This format is generally acceptable, but do not be flustered if they introduce a further name at any stage. This will be their family name.

HINDU FAITH COMMUNITY AND CUSTOMS

Core beliefs

To be reunited with God through study, devotion, prayer and service to others.

Daily acts of faith

Meditation and an act of devotion at home.

Rules of life

Three pathways (from the Bhagavad-Gita):

1. *The way of knowledge.* To cultivate knowledge by studying ancient texts.

2. *The way of action.* Deeper meditation by mind and body exercises.

3. *The way of devotion.* Expression of love for God through prayer and service.

Sanctity of life (most Hindus are vegetarians) and tolerance towards other races and religions are central to the Hindu faith.

Places of worship

- *Mandir (Hindu Temple).* This is a shrine room with the statues of Murtis (representations of the deities) with a decorated seat for the Swami (the leader of worship). Money and raw food offerings are made. Hindus dress modestly. Women will wear head coverings and all worshippers will remain silent and will sit on the floor with legs bent underneath. Males will be separated from females. Food is blessed and served to all, and is accepted with cupped hands (right hand uppermost).

- *Home.* At home, Hindus usually have a shrine where Puja (worship) takes place at dusk with prayers, bells and incense. Food is blessed,

offered to the deities and sprinkled with water. Some is put aside for unexpected visitors and birds. Hindus eat with the right hand and wash hands after the meal.

Annual events

- *Holi.* Death of winter.
- *Rama Navami.* A celebration of Rama's birth, the seventh incarnation of Vishnu.
- *Janamashtami.* Celebration of the birth of Krishna, the eighth incarnation of Vishnu.
- *Divali.* To honour the deity Lakshmi and celebrate the reunion of Rama and his wife Sita.
- *Shivaratri.* To honour the deity Shiva.

Language

In the United Kingdom the languages of English, Gujarati, Hindi, Punjabi and Bengali are used. Text is written in Sanskrit.

Dress

Women are required to cover all the body with only an occasional derogation. The Sari is a traditional dress.

Diet

Hindus are mainly vegetarians. Some refrain from consuming alcohol, onions, garlic and salt. If one was to prepare food for a Hindu, then rice, salads, vegetables or fruit should be offered.

Names

Usually there are three names. The first is the given name followed by a complimentary name (usually the father's given name or the name of the deity) and then the family caste name. For record purposes, the last name of the surname should be used – for example Ravi Rama *Patel.*

MUSLIM FAITH COMMUNITY AND CUSTOMS

Deity

Allah and the prophet Muhammed.

Core beliefs

To submit to the will of Allah, by the declaration of faith.

Rules of life

The Five pillars of Islam:

1. *Prayer five times a day.*

2. *Almsgiving to the needy and poor.*

3. *Fasting between dawn and sunset during the month of Ramadan.*

4. *Declaration of faith in Allah and Muhammed.*

5. *Pilgrimage to Mecca at least once in a lifetime (Haj).*

Daily acts of faith

- Pre-prayer ablutions.
- Prayer at dawn, mid-day, late afternoon, after sunset and late evening.

Places of worship

- *Mosque (Muslim Temple).* There is a raised pulpit for the Imam (leader of worship). Worshippers have to remove shoes, dress modestly and cover everything. Women must wear a head covering and must not visit when menstruating. Silence will be observed and all worshippers will be seated on the floor with their legs bent underneath. Males will be separated from females.

- *Home.* Worshippers will avoid mixing with unrelated members of the opposite sex. Homes will usually have pictures of holy buildings rather than pictures of the Prophet Muhammed.

Annual events

- *First of Muharram.* New year.
- *Milad-un Nabi.* Celebration of the Prophet Muhammed's birth.
- *Lailat-ul-Bara'at.* Allah decides the fate of mankind for the following year.
- *Ramadan.* Fasting from sunrise to sunset during the ninth month of the Muslim year.
- *Eid-ul Fitr.* End of Ramadan.
- *Eid-ul-Adha.* The end of the time of annual pilgrimage.

Dress

Women are generally required to cover the body with the exception of the face. Males are required to cover from waist to knee.

Diet

Muslims are religiously forbidden to eat pork or pork by-products, or to drink alcohol. They are only allowed to eat Halal meat that is killed and prepared by a Muslim according to Islamic laws. If one was to offer food, then falafel, rice salads, vegetables or fruit that is well spiced could be presented.

Names

Any number of personal and religious names may be given. They do not necessarily have to represent the family name.

BUDDHIST FAITH COMMUNITY AND CUSTOMS

Deity

Buddha (three schools).

Core beliefs

To develop kindness and awareness to all living things, to achieve freedom from suffering and seek delivery to Nirvana through incarnation.

Daily acts of faith

Meditation; displaying acts of devotion.

Rules of life

An eight-fold path:

1. *Right understanding*
2. *Right thought*
3. *Right speech*
4. *Right action*
5. *Right livelihood*
6. *Right effort*
7. *Right mindfulness*
8. *Right meditation.*

Places of worship

- *Vihara (Buddhist centre).* This has a shrine room with a statue of Buddha. Buddhists make use of candles, incense and food offerings. Worshippers must remove shoes, dress modestly, practise silence and sit on the floor.
- *Home.* This will usually have a shrine with statue, candles, incense and flowers.

Annual events

- *Wesak.* Buddha's birth
- *Full moon.* Celebrate Buddha's birth as he was born on a full moon.

Language

In the United Kingdom, English, Cantonese, Hakka, Japanese and Shinhalese are spoken. Text is written in wither Sanskrit or Pali.

Diet

Buddhists are mainly vegetarians, although some may eat fish or eggs. Some refrain from eating onions, garlic and salt. On fast days (full and new moon and festival days) food can only be eaten before noon.

Names

Buddhists usually have two names only. The first is the family name and the second the given name. This is the opposite way round way to Christians.

JEWISH FAITH COMMUNITY AND CUSTOMS

Core beliefs

To live by God's laws as revealed by Moses. The most important is to believe in and love God through prayer, study and by celebrating the yearly cycle of holy days.

Daily acts of faith

- Recite 3a daily prayer called *Shema*.
- Observe the Sabbath (sunset Friday to sunset Saturday).
- Attend Synagogue, prayers and family meals (depending upon orthodoxy).

Rules of life

The Torah, which includes the commandments:

1.   *Thou shalt have no other Gods before me.*

2.   *Thou shalt not make unto thee any graven image.*

3.   *Thou shalt not take the name of the Lord thy God in vain.*

4.   *Remember the Sabb3 false witness against thy neighbour.*

5.   *Thou shalt not covert thy neighbour's house, wife and so on.*

Place of worship

- *Synagogue (Jewish Temple)*. The Torah is kept in a covered alcove with a constantly burning lamp. It is taken from the alcove to be read from a raised platform. Worshippers will dress modestly with a head covering for women. Silence is practised and worshippers sit on the floor. Males and females are kept separate. Bread and wine are blessed and served to all. Mezuzah, a small wooden box that contains the first part of the daily prayer, is attached to the doorways.
- *Home*. Mezuzah is positioned on the right-hand doorpost of all rooms, except the toilet and bathroom.

Annual events

- *Days of Awe*. Rosh Hashanah (new year).
- *Yom Kippur*. Day of fasting.
- *Sukkot*. Wandering of children in Israel.
- *Peasach*. Exodus from Egypt.
- *Shavuot*. Receiving Torah.
- *Chankah*. Festival of light.
- *Purim*. Reminder of the story of Esther.
- *Tishah B'Av*. Commemorates the destruction of the Temple.

Language

In the United Kingdom English is spoken in the main. However, Hebrew or Yiddish may be spoken. Texts are written in Hebrew.

Dress

Women are required to cover the body with the exception of the face. Orthodox men wear skull-caps and facial hair.

Diet

Kashrut (laws governing diet) requires that kosher food must be prepared under special procedures. There will be no pork, meat and milk in the same meal. Laws extend to the utensils used in preparation as well as to the food itself.

RASTAFARIANISM

Rastafarianism is a movement inspired by Marcus Garvey in Jamaica during the 1930s. It is a way of life rather than a religion, although it has many links with Christianity and Judaism. Rastafarians regard Ras Tafari, the last emperor of Ethiopia, as the Messiah of the black race. Their beliefs are based on the Bible, especially the Old Testament, and the Book of Revelation in the New Testament. They use the language Patois, which is a regional dialect of a language – the jargon of a particular group. Rastafarians:

- Worship one God.
- Wear their hair long in dreadlocks.
- Refer to men as 'Bretherens' and women as 'Sisterens'.
- Usually keep their heads covered, women with a wrap or a tam, and men with a tam. (Tams are knitted, leather or cloth.)
- Substitute the word 'God' with 'Jah'.
- Do not eat pork and fish with scales. Many do not drink alcohol.
- View the use of marijuana as a religious rite.
- Wear items in the colours red, gold and green (colours of the Ethiopian flag) and black, which have specific meanings: red signifies the blood shed in the Rastafarian historical struggle; gold signifies faith, prosperity and sunshine; green signifies recognition of the land of Ethiopia; and black signifies the colour of the people.

DIVERSITY

Inappropriate behaviour

Rather than trying to define inappropriate behaviour, it might be better to reflect on appropriate behaviour. Appropriate behaviour could be described as any behaviour that maintains the respect for, and the dignity of, all people, regardless of any social factor such as gender, age, lifestyle, culture, race and disability, economic or social status, and so on.

Behaviour does not necessarily relate to the spoken word. Sometimes behaviour can include sneering at someone, by using a particular tone of voice or displaying particular body language. Inappropriate behaviour is behaviour that stereotypes, belittles and demeans others – behaviour that is extremely offensive.

Challenging inappropriate behaviour

It is better to challenge inappropriate behaviour sooner rather than later. An assessment needs to be made to establish whether the perpetrator is ready to be challenged. Will the challenge come as a 'bombshell' or will the perpetrator expect you to make the challenge? An early challenge might remove these concerns.

The decision must then be made as to whether the challenge should be made in public or private. Depending on the circumstances, a public challenge may have benefits. The challenge may serve as a reminder to all the people present that inappropriate behaviour will not be tolerated. The major problem is that it may embarrass the perpetrator or give rise to support for the perpetrator from other people who are present.

If the decision is made to make the challenge in private, its benefits include keeping the matter confidential, it minimises embarrassment and it raises the issue of educating the perpetrator on matters affecting culture, diversity and appropriate behaviour. It is important if the challenge is made in private that the victim is informed of the action taken. Failure to do so may lead the victim to think that nothing has happened.

RELEVANT LEGISLATION
Race Relations Act 1976

Under this Act, it is unlawful to discriminate against anyone on the grounds of race, colour, nationality (including citizenship), or ethnic or national origin. All racial groups are protected from discrimination.

Racist incidents, ranging from criminal harassment and abuse to physical violence, are outlawed under the criminal law. Such offences include inciting racial hatred, by publishing and disseminating material in the form of leaflets or media articles.

The Commission for Racial Equality has published a new statutory code of practice on racial equality in employment. It outlines employers' legal obligations under the Race Relations Act 1976, and contains general advice on developing policies to safeguard against discrimination and harassment. The code took legal effect from 6 April 2006.

Sex Discrimination Act 1975

The Sex Discrimination Act (SDA) prohibits sex discrimination against individuals in the areas of employment, education, and the provision of goods, facilities and services, and in the disposal or management of premises. It also prohibits discrimination in employment against married people. Since the Civil Partnership Act 2004 came into force on 5 December 2005, the same protection is afforded to those in a civil partnership as to those who are married. It is not unlawful to discriminate against someone because they are not married. Victimisation because someone has tried to exercise their rights under the SDA or Equal Pay Act is prohibited. The SDA applies to women and men of any age, including children. Discriminatory advertisements are unlawful but only the Equal Opportunities Commission can take action against advertisers.

The SDA applies to England, Wales and Scotland. There are special provisions in the SDA prohibiting harassment in employment. Harassment is defined as either:

- unwanted conduct on the grounds of the recipient's sex; or
- unwanted verbal, non-verbal or physical conduct of a sexual nature.

In either case the conduct must have the purpose, or the effect of violating the recipient's dignity, or of creating an intimidating, hostile, degrading, humiliating or offensive environment for the recipient. It is also harassment to treat somebody less favourably because they have rejected or submitted to either type of harassment described above.

Disability Discrimination Act 1995

The Disability Discrimination Act (DDA) protects disabled people in:

- employment;
- access to goods, facilities and services;
- the management, buying or renting of land or property;
- education.

Some sections became law for employers in December 1996, while others have been introduced over time:

- Since December 1996, it has been unlawful to treat disabled people less favourably than other people for a reason related to their disability.

- Since October 1999, service providers and employers have had to make reasonable adjustments for disabled people, such as providing extra help or making changes to the way they provide their services.

- Since October 2004, service providers and employers have had to make reasonable adjustments to the physical features of their premises to overcome physical barriers to access.

Additionally, the Disability Discrimination Act 2005 amends the 1995 Act to place a duty on public bodies to promote equality of opportunity for disabled people.

23 Drugs Awareness

Drugs, including alcohol, are substances that alter the way in which the body or mind works. Drugs can be defined as those controlled under the Misuse of Drugs Act 1971, prescribed drugs, over the counter medications and alcohol.

Employers should be aware that drug use is an issue for the whole workforce, and should not be thought of as more or less prevalent among employees of a certain grade, status or job type. No employer is immune to the problem. The majority of individuals who use illicit drugs or have an alcohol problem are in employment and, particularly in the early stages, the issue may go unnoticed by colleagues. Inappropriate use of drugs and alcohol can result in serious consequences for both individuals and businesses. Therefore, employers are advised to take proactive measures to address the issues of drugs and alcohol in the workplace. Developing an effective drug and alcohol policy can help clarify the organisation's rules and procedures for dealing with the issue of drugs and alcohol in a fair, consistent and supportive manner.

The huge amounts of cannabis, cocaine, heroin and other narcotics regularly seized by Customs and Excise and the police reflect the growth of the problem of drug abuse in our society. Indeed, recent research shows that out of every ten people convicted of theft and burglary in the criminal courts, eight are heroin users.

Security interest lies in the propensity of the addict among employees to steal to pay for drugs and in the consequences of addiction – progressive deterioration in:

- performance
- appearance
- behaviour
- attendance
- regard for safety.

In retail establishments, shopping precincts, hotels and the like, the presence of drug-affected people has adverse financial consequences in that the reputation of the company may be damaged, resulting in the law-abiding majority of customers taking their business elsewhere.

The first indication of a problem of drug abuse in the workplace might be the type of conversations heard. Drug users have their own terminology, and the types of drugs used have their own slang words too. Examples include:

- cannabis – hash, skunk, weed, draw;

- heroin – smack;

- amphetamines – speed;

- cocaine – snow, crack.

SIGNS OF DRUG MISUSE

Signs of drugs misuse include the presence of syringes, silver foil, burnt spoons and cardboard 'roaches', which are used as filters when smoking. Physical signs of drug abuse may include the following:

- A disregard for personal hygiene.

- Empty pill bottles or used syringes in rubbish bins or waste baskets, empty glue or solvent containers in recessed doorways or out-of-sight locations.

- Increased pilferage.

- Unusual smells in lifts, washrooms and rest rooms.

- Out of character behaviour, emotionally or in job performance by employees, including a sudden change coupled with abrupt transitions from depression to euphoria. The latter may be seen after visits to toilets – ill going in, revitalised coming out.

- Persons smelling of glue or solvents, displaying violent or irrational behaviour, wandering in a daze or in a seemingly drunken state.

- Individuals frequenting a particular public area, perhaps at particular times and being approached by others separately and briefly, possibly furtively, with a transmission of something between them (any suspicion that a 'pusher' is in operation should be notified to the police).

TYPES OF DRUGS MISUSED

The symptoms shown by a person behaving oddly may be an indication of the type of drug being used.

Marijuana

This is a derivative of the hemp plant – cannabis and hashish are from the same source and have similar effects. It is usually smoked in home-made cigarettes that are rolled and crimped at the ends. The smell of burning rope is characteristic, and users may gather in groups passing a cigarette around between them. The drug produces excitement, talkativeness, bursts of laughter, reduced physical and mental control, uncoordinated movement and subsequently drowsiness and lassitude.

Depressants

Depressants (like barbiturates) produce the effects of intoxication without the smell of liquor on the breath. Users may have slurred speech, staggering walk, confused thinking and may fall asleep.

Stimulants

These include amphetamines and cocaine, and cause abnormal physical activity, such as sweating, excitement, irritability and dilated pupils. Users may have unusual and noticeable bad breath, chapped or cracked lips, and their excessive nervous activity may lead to itching, chain smoking and talkativeness.

The drugs are usually in the form of a white powder, which can be sniffed or injected, but cocaine, 'cut' (mixed) with other substances and in pieces the size of raisins ('rocks') is smoked in pipes or burnt on tinfoil as 'crack'. A further variation is known as 'Ecstasy' or 'Es', which takes the form of vari-coloured, unglazed tablets or capsules.

Hallucinogens

Hallucinogens of the LSD type cause a trance or dreamlike state and have a common symptom – dilated pupils. Unpredictable mental effects (possibly exhilaration, panic at imagined dangers or the urge to self-destruct) are common extremes of behaviour and these may reoccur long after the drug has been taken. LSD is often supplied on tiny impregnated squares of paper, which may carry coloured designs or pictures of cartoon characters.

Opiates

Opiates like morphine and heroin or codeine are the most addictive drugs and can kill by overdose. Slurred speech, drowsiness, hallucinations and euphoria are the outward effects. Injection by syringe is the most common method, and will cause needle marks at the location of injection, which is associated with collapsed veins after prolonged use. The user will try to cover these marks by always wearing long sleeves whatever the weather. Sunglasses may also be worn to conceal dilated or pinpoint pupils. Burnt bottle tops or spoons may be found, which indicate the drug having been vaporised for inhalation.

As mentioned earlier, suspicion of drug abuse by employees on or off the premises, or of the premises being used by addicts, must be reported at once to management. The problem of drug misuse is sufficiently widespread and publicised for most companies to have established guidelines on the action to take.

LEGISLATION

The statute law in respect of drugs is the Misuse of Drugs Act 1971. The Act categorises drugs in classes:

- *Class A*. Heroin, cocaine, diamorphine, opium, methadone, prepared magic mushrooms.
- *Class B*. Amphetamines, dihydrocodeine.
- *Class C*. Diazepam, cannabis, cannabis resin and ketamine.

The main offences of interest to the security office will be those of possession. Section 5 of the Misuse of Drugs Act 1971 makes it an offence to unlawfully possess a controlled drug, or to possess a controlled drug (lawfully or not) with intent to unlawfully supply it.

There is an immediate implication here for someone who finds drugs, say secreted in toilets, because the moment they possess it, technically they are committing an offence. However, there is a defence to this. Where a person knowing or suspecting it to be a controlled drug takes possession:

- in order to prevent an offence, providing that person, as soon as possible, took reasonable steps to destroy the drugs or hand them to a person who is lawfully entitled to possess them, or

- providing that person, as soon as possible, took reasonable steps to give the drugs to a person lawfully entitled to possess them, then no offence is committed. If a security officer finds drugs, it is recommended that they hand them to a police officer as soon as is reasonably possible. If they do this they will not commit an offence. In the event of drugs being found, a notebook entry should be made that includes the time, date, location and the circumstances of their finding.

DRUG MISUSE AND UNCONSCIOUSNESS

The following procedure must be followed:

- Call the police and ambulance services.
- Render first aid if appropriate and safe to do so, ensuring personal protection from contamination by wearing protective gloves and using specialist appliances to undertake artificial respiration.
- Protect the scene of the incident until the emergency services arrive.
- Obtain details of any witnesses to the incident.
- Assist the emergency services as directed.
- Complete a note book entry as soon as possible.

24 Door Supervisors

A door supervisor is defined as 'any person employed at or near the entrance to premises to ascertain or satisfy themselves as to the suitability of members of the public to be allowed on the premises, or any person employed to maintain order on the premises'.

To avoid repeating information from other chapters, this chapter will not include all the reading material needed to give the prospective door supervisor the information required to pass the Level 2 National Certificate for Door Supervisors. What it will do is point the reader to other chapters that contain the relevant information. Where the information is not available in other chapters, it will be included here.

The Security Industry Authority (SIA) regulates and oversees the private security industry in England and Wales, and is responsible for the licensing of door supervisors. (More information about the work of the SIA can be found in Chapter 25.)

DOOR SUPERVISOR LICENCE

Since early 2004, the licensing of door supervisors has been phased in, and now a person can only work as a door supervisor if they possess an SIA licence. A person requires a Door Supervisor Licence if they are responsible for security, protection or screening the suitability of people entering the premises or dealing with conflict in pubs, clubs and other licensed premises open to the public. This applies to those specific times when alcohol is being supplied for consumption on the premises and/or regulated entertainment is taking place.

Licensed premises

The definition of 'licensed premises' includes those with:

- Premises licences (issued under the Licensing Act 2003) that authorise the supply of alcohol and/or regulated entertainment.
- Temporary event notices (issued under the Licensing Act 2003) that authorise the supply of alcohol and/or regulated entertainment.
- Licences of a prescribed description under any prescribed local statutory provision.

The definition of 'licensed premises' *does not* include:

- Premises with a club premises certificate issued under the Licensing Act 2003.
- Premises authorised for regulated entertainment within the meaning of paragraph 2(1)(a) or (b) of Schedule 1 of the Licensing Act 2003 (plays and films).
- Premises with a licence in effect under Part 2 of the Gaming Act 1968.

Obtaining a door supervisor licence

To obtain a licence, three requirements have to be satisfied:

1. The applicant must pass an identity check.
2. The applicant must pass a Criminal Records Bureau check.
3. The applicant must possess a recognised door supervision qualification.

RECOGNISED QUALIFICATIONS

The SIA has invited the awarding bodies of the British Institute of Innkeeping, the City and Guilds and the Northern College of Further Education to work together in support of the Door Supervisor Licence. To this end, the Level 2 National Certificate for Door Supervisors has been created. If a person does not have a recognised door supervision qualification, they will have to complete this course of training before a licence will be granted. In addition, they will have to pass two examinations to satisfy the examiners that they have the necessary knowledge to practise as a door supervisor.

Where a person already holds a door supervisor qualification, that person may be fully or partially exempt from taking the Level 2 qualifications. The conditions of exemptions are:

- If the door supervisor has been awarded Stage 1 and 2 of the British Institute of Innkeeping's door supervision qualification after 1 January 2001, he or she will have full exemption.
- If the door supervisor has been awarded one of the qualifications of the Northern College of Further Education, The Security Industry Training Organisation or the National Open College Network since the 1 January 2001, he or she will be able to use this qualification to obtain partial exemption.

The door supervision local authority, British Innkeeping Association and Northern College of Further Education qualifications that were available before 2005 are no longer acceptable and have been replaced by the Level 2 qualifications. (The full details of the exemptions and other useful information for door supervisors can be found on the SIA's website at www.the-sia.org.uk.)

LEVEL 2 NATIONAL CERTIFICATE FOR DOOR SUPERVISORS

This qualification consists of two mandatory units:

- Unit 1: The roles and responsibilities of door supervisors.
- Unit 2: Conflict management for door supervisors.

The syllabus for Unit 1 of the qualification consists of:

- behavioural standards
- civil and criminal law
- searching
- arrest
- drugs awareness
- recording incidents and crime scene preservation
- licensing law
- health and safety at work
- emergency procedures.

The syllabus for Unit 2 of the qualification consists of:

- Introduction to communication skills and conflict management.
- Application of communication skills and conflict management.

UNIT 1

Aim

The aim of Unit 1 is to introduce the trainee to the leisure and security industry. It does this by encouraging the trainee to meet the following objectives:

- Define the role of the door supervisor.
- Identify the qualities of the door supervisor.
- Identify the key players in the leisure and security industry.
- State the relationships with the SIA, the police and the local authority.
- State the main objectives of door supervisors.
- State the requirements for door supervisors under the Private Security Industry Act 2001.

Behavioural standards

Appearance, manner and professionalism are important requirements for door supervisors. The best door supervisors go about their work in a polite, quietly efficient and professional manner, are smartly dressed and good mannered.

When seeking entry to licensed premises, the door supervisor is often the first person to be seen. Appearance and professionalism will reflect on the management of the premises and its reputation for good customer service. Therefore, there is no place within this area of work for the over-zealous, prejudiced individual who has no regard for the rights of others. Indeed, this type of individual may affect the numbers of people likely to attend the premises, harm relationships with the police and, ultimately, affect the profitability of the business.

Civil and criminal law

The civil and criminal law relevant to door supervisors is discussed in Chapters 8 and 9. The civil law of trespass may also become relevant to the licensee or manager of licensed premise. Trespass occurs when a person enters premises in possession of another person without any express or implied permission to do so. Express is where permission from a person is given, and implied is where it is accepted that people are freely allowed to enter premises without express permission – for example, someone entering a supermarket.

It is not unusual for licensed premises to require a person to be searched as a condition of entry. The method of search is discussed later. If a person refuses permission to be searched they should not be allowed entry. If subsequently, by some means that person enters the premises, the person becomes a trespasser and, under common law, may be ejected by using a reasonable degree of force.

However, before using force the trespasser must be asked to leave the premises and be given a reasonable time to do so peaceably. The same applies to the ejection of someone who has been allowed entry to the premises where offences contrary to the licensing laws are being committed or where it may affect the licensee's ability to maintain an orderly house.

The amount of force permissible must be commensurate with the amount of harm likely to otherwise result, but may not include a beating, wounding or other physical injury. An explanation of the use of force in respect of an arrest is included in Chapter 10.

Searching

Information regarding the searching of people and the conduct of the search is contained in Chapter 12. Note, however, that no person other than the police has a right to search without permission. If consent is not given to a search, the person should be refused entry to the premises. Where suspected drugs or offensive weapons are found, the police should be informed. There is important information about offensive weapons in Chapter 21 and about drugs awareness in Chapter 23 (in particular with regards to the possession of drugs after seizure).

Arrest

The powers and procedures in relation to arrest by persons other than the police can be found in Chapter 10.

Drugs awareness

Information in relation to drugs awareness is set out in Chapter 23.

Recording incidents and crime scene preservation

Information about recording incidents can be found in Chapter 14, and preserving a crime scene is discussed in Chapter 19.

Licensing law

The Licensing Act 2003 provides for a unified system of regulation of licensable activities that include:

- the sale and supply of alcohol;
- the provision of regulated entertainment;
- the provision of late night refreshment.

Licensing authorities

The licensing function has now been moved from Licensing Justices to:

- In England, the district council, or the county council where no district council exists.
- In Wales, the county council or the county borough council.
- In London, the London borough councils, the Common Council of the City of London, the sub-treasurer of the Inner Temple or the under-treasurer of the Middle Temple.
- In the Scilly Isles, the Council of the Isles of Scilly.

The licensing authority must carry out its functions under the Licensing Act with a view to promoting, in the public interest:

- the prevention of crime and disorder;
- public safety;
- the prevention of public nuisance;
- the protection of children from harm.

Alcohol

Alcohol means spirits, wine, beer, cider or any other fermented, distilled or spirituous liquor, but does not include:

- alcohol, strength not exceeding 0.5 per cent at the time of the sale or supply;

- perfume;
- flavouring essences not consumed as or with dutiable alcoholic liquor;
- alcohol contained in a medicinal product;
- liqueur confectionery.

Premises

Premises means any place and includes vehicles intended or adapted for use on roads, vessels including a ship, boat or raft, and movable structures.

Licences

A personal licence is granted to an individual authorising that person to supply or authorise the supply of alcohol in accordance with the premises licence. A personal license must be held by a person who is responsible for the day-to-day running of the premises. There may be more than one personal licence holder and any sale of alcohol must be made under the authority of the personal licence holder. The police may require the licence holder to produce the licence for examination, where the licensee is on the licensed premises or where the licensee is on premises where there is a temporary event notice in force.

A premises licence is granted by a licensing authority to a person or body in respect of premises, authorising them to be used for one or more licensable activities.

Police rights of entry

A constable may, if necessary using reasonable force, enter and search any premises in respect of which he or she has reason to believe that an offence under the Licensing Act 2003 has been, is being or is about to be committed. This power is extended to clubs where there is a club premises certificate in force and to premises where there is a temporary event permit in force.

Licensing act offences

Young people

It is an offence for any person to:

- Sell alcohol to a person under the age of 18.

- Knowingly allow the sale or supply of alcohol on relevant premises to a person under 18 years.

It is an offence for a person under 18 years to:

- Buy or attempt to buy alcohol.
- Knowingly consume alcohol on relevant premises.

It is an offence for a person to:

- Buy or attempt to buy alcohol on behalf of a person who is under 18 years of age.
- Knowingly allow the consumption of alcohol on relevant premises by a person aged under 18.

Drunk and disorderly conduct

It is an offence for any person on relevant premises to knowingly:

- Allow disorderly conduct on relevant premises.
- Sell or attempt to sell alcohol to a person who is drunk, or allow alcohol to be sold to such a person.

These offences apply to:

- Any person who works on the premises in a paid or unpaid capacity authorised to prevent the conduct or sell alcohol.
- The premises licence holder or designated supervisor.
- The premises user in relation to a temporary event user.

There are another two offences that relate to the door supervisor:

- It is an offence for a person on relevant premises to knowingly obtain or attempt to obtain alcohol for consumption on those premises by a drunken person.
- It is an offence for a person who is drunk and disorderly without reasonable excuse to fail to leave relevant premises when requested to do so or to enter or attempt to enter relevant premises when requested not to do so by: (a) a constable; (b) any person who works at the premises in a paid or unpaid capacity authorised to make the request; (c) the premises licence holder or the designated premises supervisor; (d) where a club premises certificate is in effect, any member or officer of the club present on the premises at the

time in a capacity enabling him or her to make the request; or (e) the premises user in relation to a temporary event notice.

Health and safety at work

Information in relation to health and safety can be found in Chapter 17.

Emergency procedures

Information on emergency procedures is discussed in Chapter 19.

UNIT 2

Aims

* To discuss communication skills and conflict management.
* To observe and discuss scenario situations requiring effective communication and conflict management.

Conflict management

Information in relation to conflict management and resolution can be found in Chapter 21.

25

The SIA, Professional Standards and Further Education

THE SECURITY INDUSTRY AUTHORITY (SIA)

The SIA exists to manage the licensing of the private security industry as provided for in the Private Security Industry Act 2001. It also aims to raise standards of professionalism and skills within the private security industry and to promote and spread best practice. The SIA is the only authority in England and Wales dealing with these private security issues and it reports directly to the Home Secretary.

Licensing of the security industry

A key role for the SIA involves the managing and issuing of licences for people working in particular areas of the private security business. The current designated sectors or activities that must be covered by a licence are as follows:

- Door supervisors, both in-house and supplied under contract.
- Vehicle immobilisers on private land, both in-house and supplied under contract.
- Security guards supplied under contract.
- Keyholders supplied under contract.
- Close protection operatives supplied under contract.
- Cash and valuables in transit operatives supplied under contract.
- CCTV (public space surveillance) operatives supplied under contract.

There are two types of licence:

- *Front-line licence* – for door supervisors.
- *Non-front-line licence* – for managers, supervisors and directors or partners of security companies.

The front-line licence is a badge that must be worn where it can be seen when working; the non-front-line licence is a letter that must be kept and (if required) produced for inspection by authorised personnel.

If a person has a non-front-line door supervisor licence, they will not need to get another non-front-line licence if they are involved in another area of licensable activity. Any SIA licence, whether front-line or non-front-line, allows security staff to act as a keyholder.

The cost of a licence is subject to increase when conditions and time permits. However, once paid, the fee covers licensing for a three-year period.

FURTHER EDUCATION AND TRAINING

While private security has expanded in terms of remit and professional profile, it has not yet consolidated its position in terms of professional and vocational qualifications. Within the United Kingdom, a number of security qualifications exist but these tend to be awarded in isolation by individual organisations or professional bodies, or are qualifications that are accredited by any number of accreditation bodies.

The SIA recognises that it is essential for all personnel involved in the security industry to have undergone a structured programme of training and education resulting in recognised qualifications if they are to be effective and professional in their role. Increasingly, industry stakeholders also recognise that individuals with enforcement responsibilities must have a broad range of skills and a clear understanding of their role. As the scope, diversity and importance of their work continues to grow, so the degree of professionalism expected from those involved in the security industry will increase.

PERSONAL INTEGRITY

It goes without saying that a person employed in security work must not only be, but must be seen to be, strictly fair and honest. The status of security officer allows access and opportunities beyond those of other employees, and trust in the integrity of security staff is essential to the employer. It must be emphasised that there can be no considerations of loyalty when a colleague is to be found abusing that trust.

As part of the vetting process, people now entering the security industry have to undergo Criminal Records Bureau checks before employment is considered. In addition, prospective employers of security staff may ask applicants to supply proof that they have no convictions. This is provided for by Section 21 of the Data Protection Act 1984, which, subject to certain exceptions, gives an individual the right to be supplied with personal data held by the police. Information about the application form to be completed is available at most main police stations. Proof of identity will be required when the application is submitted.

ROLE OF SUPERVISORS IN MAINTAINING STANDARDS

Training can impart the knowledge and instruction needed for a professional approach to the job, but it is the immediate supervisor's job to see it put into practice.

Supervisors will be acting under orders and must know exactly what is expected of them and what is expected of the team. If the supervisor has the slightest doubt, clarification must be sought before the team is briefed; what ensues is the responsibility of the supervisor. Much will be purely repetitive routine, but even then each member of the team has to be clear about what the job is, how they will go about it and any time factors involved. In the case of contract security, the briefing might have to cover detailed plans of unfamiliar premises and instructions on reporting incidents. The briefing might also include details of special risks and other material features, including the client's own rules and emergency procedures.

On-the-job visiting and checking follows, and good supervisors will take the opportunity to learn more about team members, assessing enthusiasm, knowledge, giving advice, answering queries and, in effect, continuing the training process. Where a disciplinary matter arises, action must be fair and impartial, but firm – the true and hardest test of supervisory competence.

Newly appointed supervisors must accept that they are no longer just a member of the team but the member responsible for the way the team performs. A division has been created and the respect of the other members of the team is necessary. This can be demonstrated by:

- displaying competence;
- a willingness to make decisions;
- a willingness to accept responsibility;
- displaying enthusiasm for the job;
- adaptability in the face of the unexpected;

- ability to criticise without belittling;
- standing up for subordinates in the face or unfair criticism or complaint;
- exercising common sense and fairness in listening to valid suggestions and comments.

The ability to produce, and assist them in producing, clear and concise reports will be appreciated by subordinates. Good supervisors provide the backbone of the job, and much of the professionalism.

Appendix: Professional Bodies

THE SECURITY INDUSTRY AUTHORITY (SIA)

PO Box 9
Newcastle-Upon-Tyne NE82 6YX
Telephone: 08702 430100

JOINT SECURITY INDUSTRY COUNCIL

1 Queen Anne's Gate
Westminster
London SW1H 9BT
Telephone: 020 7227 3599

INTERNATIONAL INSTITUTE OF SECURITY

Suite 8, The Business Centre
57 Torquay Road
Paignton
Devon TQ3 3DT
Telephone: 01803 663275

INTERNATIONAL PROFESSIONAL SECURITY ASSOCIATION

Northumberland House
11 The Pavement
Popes Lane
Ealing
London W5 4NG
Telephone: 020 8832 7417

INSTITUTE OF PROFESSIONAL INVESTIGATORS

Bank House
81 St Judes Road
Englefield Green
Egham
Surrey TW20 0DF
Telephone: 0870 330 8622

Index

About the Author

David Brooksbank is a recently retired police officer who has completed 30 years service with West Yorkshire Police. For a number of years he was a crime prevention officer.

He is the sole proprietor of David Brooksbank Training, a small training organisation that delivers bespoke training in security practice, conflict resolution, basic criminal law, personal safety, lone working, and health and safety (www.davidbrooksbanktraining.co.uk). He is a training consultant for a number of colleges of further education and has written course and training materials for these and other organisations. He is a distance learning tutor for the International Institute of Security's City and Guilds distance learning programmes in security management, and has provided training for a number of organisations including those specialising in manned guarding, the NHS, retail enterprises, local authorities, leisure and tourism companies and museums.

David is a respected public speaker and has spoken at a number of conferences. His keynote speech – 'In the Presence of Danger' – is a unique personal safety training experience based on perception, intuition and prediction as a means of identifying the survival signals that protect us from violence; an experience that is designed to stimulate personal safety responses in lone workers (those people who work away from their company base, such as community nurses, company representatives and so on).

David has a BA (Honours) in Education and Training (University of Huddersfield), a Certificate of Education and is a post-graduate of the University of the West of England, where he studied Crime Prevention and Community Safety. He is a fellow of the International Institute of Security.

**If you have found this book useful you may be interested
in other titles from Gower**

**Accounting Irregularities in Financial Statements:
A Definitive Guide for Litigators, Auditors and Fraud Investigators**
Benny Kwok
978-0-566-08621-2

**Complete Guide to Business Risk Management
Second Edition**
Kit Sadgrove
978-0-566-08661-8

**Corporate Fraud
Third Edition**
Michael J. Comer
978-0-566-07810-1

**Fraud and Corruption in Public Services:
A Guide to Risk and Prevention**
Peter Jones
978-0-566-08566-6

**Fraud and Corruption:
Detection and Prevention**
Nigel Iyer and Martin Samociuk
978-0-566-08699-1

**Deception at Work:
Investigating and Countering Lies and Fraud Strategies**
Michael J. Comer and Timothy E. Stephens
978-0-566-08636-6

**Information Security and Employee Behaviour:
How to Reduce Risk Through Employee Education, Training and
Awareness**
Angus McIlwraith
978-0-566-08647-2

Information Risk and Security:
Preventing and Investigating Workplace Computer Crime
Edward Wilding
978-0-566-08685-4

Investigating Corporate Fraud
Michael J. Comer
978-0-566-08531-4

Money Laundering:
A Concise Guide for All Business
Doug Hopton
978-0-566-08639-7

Purchasing Scams and How to Avoid Them
Trevor Kitching
978-0-566-08281-8

Risk-Based Auditing
Phil Griffiths
978-0-566-08652-6

For further information on these and all our titles visit our
website – www.gowerpub.com
All online orders receive a discount

GOWER